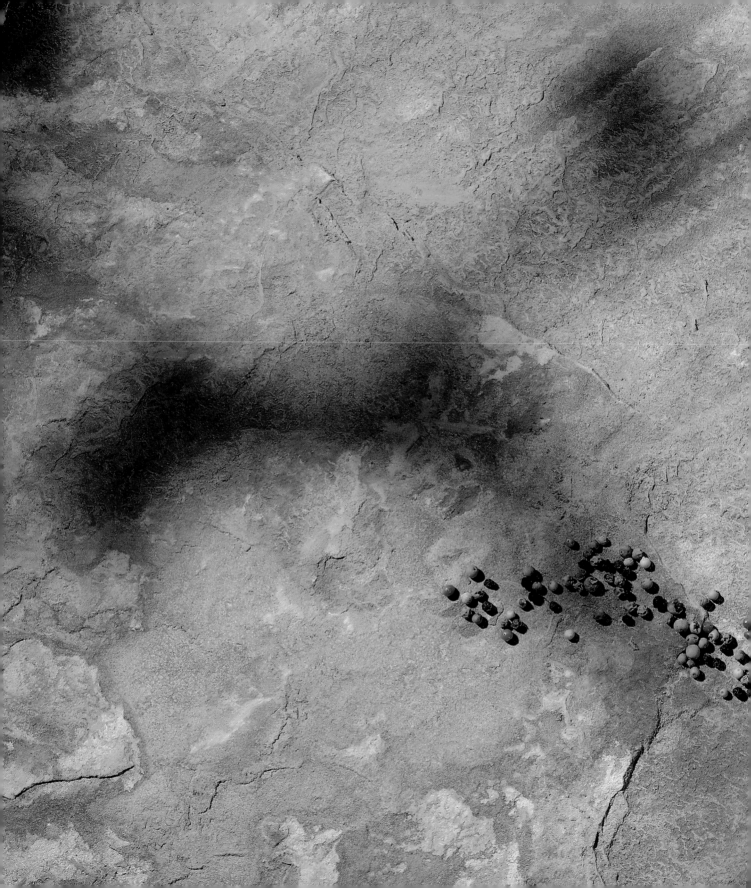

The President's Choice
Barbecue Cookbook

THE PRESIDENT'S CHOICE
BARBECUE COOKBOOK

150 Great Tastes of Summer

Copyright © 1995 Loblaw Companies Limited.
All rights reserved.
Published and produced in Canada by Loblaw Companies Limited.
Color separations by Praven Graphic Productions Inc.
Printed in Canada by Thorn Press Limited.

Canadian Cataloguing in Publication Data
White, Carol Ann
        The President's Choice barbecue cookbook : 150 great tastes of summer
Includes index.
ISBN 0-9697259-1-4
1. Barbecue cookery.   I. Litwin, Frances J.   II. Loblaw Companies Limited.
III. Title.
TX840.B3W53 1995   641.5'784   C95-900072-0

Recipes for this book were tested on electric and gas grills. Charcoal grills may produce different results. Grilling times will vary with the cut of meat, grill position, weather, coal temperature and degree of doneness desired.

Grateful acknowledgement is made for permission to reprint the following:

Page 50: Excerpt from "The Highly Probable Future" by Joseph Coates reproduced with permission by *The Futurist*, published by the World Future Society, 7910 Woodmont Ave., Suite 450, Bethesda, Maryland 20814, tel: (301) 656-8274.

Page 52: Excerpt from "Rustic Renaissance" from *Traveller's Guide to the Food of Italy* by Valentina Harris, copyright © 1988. By permission of Henry Holt and Company, Inc.

Page 53: Excerpt from "Song to Barbecue Sauce" from *One Fell Soup: Or I'm Just A Bug On The Windshield Of Life* by Roy Blount Jr., copyright © 1975. First appeared in Eastern Airlines' *Pastimes*. By permission of Little, Brown and Company.

Page 100: Excerpt from *The Thrill of the Grill* by Chris Schlesinger and John Willoughby, copyright © 1990, published by William Morrow and Company, Inc.

Page 172: Miss Manners reprinted by permission of United Feature Syndicate.

Page 258: "Salt Spring Punch" from *Salt Spring Island Cooking* by Rodney Polden and Pamela Thornley, copyright © 1993. By permission of Macmillan Canada.

Product Availability
PC, President's Choice and President's Blend products are available in Canada at Loblaws, Loblaws Superstores, Supercentres, St. Clair Market, Zehrs, Food Plus Markets from Zehrs, no frills, mr. grocer, valu-mart, freshmart, Your Independent Grocer, Fortinos, the real Canadian Superstore, Extra Foods, O.K. Economy, Lucky Dollar, Super Value, Shop Easy, Atlantic Superstores, Atlantic SuperValu, Save Easy, Atlantic Grocer, Dominion Newfoundland. Please note that some products featured in this book may not be available at all stores. For questions concerning specific products, contact the manager of the store nearest you.

Contents

DIRECTOR OF PHOTOGRAPHY: RUSS RUDD
EDITOR: CAROL WHITE
WRITER: FRANCES LITWIN
ART DIRECTION/DESIGN: RONY ZIBARA
PHOTOGRAPHY: DOUG BRADSHAW
PRIMARY RECIPE DEVELOPMENT: ALISON JARVEST
RECIPE DEVELOPMENT: TED READER
PRODUCTION ARTIST: LINDA BOZEK
PROOFREADER: JANET HINGSBERG
FOOD STYLISTS: CLAIRE STANCER, OLGA TRUCHAN
AND JENNIFER MCLAGAN
PROPS COORDINATOR: JANET WALKINSHAW
PRODUCTION DIRECTOR: R.W. POHLAK & ASSOC. INC.

INTRODUCTION

The only kind of equality that counts is being equal to the occasion.

— old range saying

The sound of food sizzling and flames whooshing when fat hits fire. The mineral fragrances of earth and wind mixing with the mouthwatering aromas of food as it chars over smoldering coals. The acrid haze of smoke that stings your eyes and catches your breath when it billows out from a lifted lid. This is barbecue.

Barbecuing forces us to see, hear, smell, feel, taste and experience food in the most intimate way. As you leaf through these pages, we hope you'll discover why barbecue aficionados believe that they belong to a secret society. They don't. They only think they do because of the profound way in which barbecuing engages the senses.

Anyone who can light a fire can barbecue, although there are certain techniques that go beyond basic char and spill over into finesse. So we asked our esteemed gurus of the grill — in this case, our captive recipe development chefs and seasoned barbecue friends — to tell us what goes into good barbecue. "Give us every last detail."

We found out what single cut of meat can satisfy a multiplicity of tastes from rare to well done (p. 86). We discovered how to make the cross-char markings on steaks that are the sign of a professional grill chef (p. 60). We learned how to tell when a steak is done by touch alone (p. 62) and a foolproof way to cook salmon (p. 167).

We've passed along all these essential secrets, plus the ones you've always suspected your barbecue friends were keeping to themselves, in this, *The President's Choice Barbecue Cookbook: 150 Great Tastes of Summer.* They're each identified by a small "barbecue flame" to help you spot them at a glance.

What's more, we've assumed (as we did in our first President's Choice cookbook) that you have neither the time nor inclination to spend long hours fussing in the kitchen. So the more than 150 recipes in this summer collection — including our selection of recipes from 10 top chefs (see p.138) — are not only foolproof, but fast. Each dish incorporates President's Choice products, which simplify preparation while delivering a sophistication of taste. It's like having your own sous chef to assist with mealtime preparation!

To initiates of this celebratory rite of summer, or those who love good food but don't have much opportunity to cook, we offer this preliminary advice: Tread carefully around an experienced *chef de gril*. Something comes over people who have inhaled too much mesquite smoke. You may be dealing with an alter ego that's inclined to overstate the effort that goes into preparing delicious char cuisine. (Hence this book.) They'll intimate that barbecuing requires constant, dedicated practice in the most gruelling — or did they say grilling? — of circumstances. They'll say it demands a natural born instinct. Uh-huh.

You've probably heard it all before. We know we have: The trial by fire that is at the very heart of barbecue. The fact is, barbecuing is easy. It doesn't even require expensive sophisticated equipment. The Mongol hordes dismounted for barbecues in their sweep of central Asia in the 14th century. Not only were these ancient warriors accomplished horsemen and archers, but it seems they were also inventive trail cooks. They'd heat their iron helmets (some say shields) over an open fire and cook their food on the red-hot rounded crowns. Similar instances of ingenuity are not difficult to find. In France, for example, archeologists pried apart two rocks to find the remains of a charred bird sandwiched in between, proving that even two suitably shaped stones, heated red hot, are adequate for the job. (The unsolved mystery here is whether the blackened bird was deliberately rejected for being inedible or simply forgotten by the hunter-cook.)

You may prefer a barbecue with all the bells and whistles, but it really does not matter whether you use a hibachi — Japanese for "firebox" — with a surface just large enough to hold two beef patties, a conventional kettle grill or a fancy gas barbecue. Eventually, you will learn how to start a fire with your equipment and how to maintain it, how to gauge the heat it generates with the lid up or down, and how long to cook your favorite foods. Ultimately, barbecue is a matter of taste. It's the gratifying sensations of char and sauce and crust and juice that are the reward when you finally sink your teeth into that first forkful.

This may be a good place to settle some terminology. Throughout this cookbook, we have used the word "barbecue" interchangeably with "grilling." They are, to be precise, two distinct concepts. Barbecue means long cooking over slow heat. Grilling is fast cooking over intense flame. Siblings of Promethean origin, they both define outdoor cooking in their own fashion.

Pit cooking, a technique practised by indigenous peoples, gave rise to what many devotees of grill cooking recognize today as barbecue. What it amounts to essentially is meat in a hole. That may be a rough way to treat food, but it's about as close to the land as eating can get. In Australia, along shorelines, creeks and open grasslands, there are many old aboriginal ground ovens — "cooking places" — to which people can return time and again.

The motto for this kind of barbecue — aka barbeque, barbie cue, BBQ, bar-b-q or just plain Q, however you choose to spell it — is "cook it slow and cook it low." The first rule of pluperfect barbecue is that the food stay on the grill for interminably long periods with nary a sizzle, the darkening crust moistened by the natural juices that ooze upward and quietly erupt on the surface; the meat irrevocably reaching in this absolute stillness of heat and smoke what one pit boss calls "a higher plane of existence." Economical and flavorful cuts such as beef brisket and pork ribs benefit greatly from this long, slow cooking (some call it long, slow smoking).

Unfortunately, this is hardly the kind of barbecue that lends itself to an activity-packed schedule, unless you're the kind of person who'd enjoy jury-rigging the requisite equipment from an old oil drum or a couple of bathtubs (useful when hinged) and you have the hours it takes to slow-cook at temperatures hovering around 200°F (100°C).

No, you'll find no slow cooking in this book. Our President's Choice recipes call for grilling: Cooking with intense heat and smoke. As a result, the emphasis is on quick-cooking everything from appetizers to main dishes and even grilled desserts. Depending on your barbecue unit, cooking temperatures will range from medium (350°F/180°C) to high (500°F/260°C).

Nevertheless, we have included oven-cooked versions of two genuine barbecue delicacies: Carolina-style Pulled Pork Sandwich (p. 197), which

tradition dictates must be served with coleslaw in a soft white hamburger bun — this is the famous "pig sandwich" celebrated at marathon barbecues such as the three-day Memphis in May competition (more about that on p. 100) — and hickory-flavored Texas Brisket Sandwich (p. 196), just as tasty but a lot more convenient to prepare than the authentic version, which can require the services of a Caterpillar just to dig the pit.

When it comes right down to it, the art of fast-cook barbecue can be summed up in five words:

• **Blazemanship.** Thomas Edison chalked up success to 10% inspiration and 90% sweat. (Sometimes the ratio feels more like 1 to 99.) The ability to tend the fire is at least 90% of barbecuing. It includes such mundane chores as starting the fire, controlling the flames, making whatever adjustments are necessary to maintain the heat, and making sure you don't run out of fuel. It also means maintaining your equipment for efficiency and safety.

• **Appetite.** Eating outdoors always builds a healthy appetite. And since there's no greater stimulant to the appetite than fresh air — the amount of food that can be packed away when one eats alfresco is astounding — always plan on providing more food than usual.

• **Timing.** A very important element. Prepare side dishes ahead of time, not when you see how lonely those grilled lamb chops look on the plate. That way, you avoid running between patio and kitchen and the risk of having nothing turn out right.

• **Pacing.** Allow anticipation to build. To mute hunger pangs before the main event, serve simple snacks or hors d'oeuvres, or grill up small eats such as sausages, vegetable slices and President's Choice Rustico bread.

• **Bravado.** Be daring. Nothing succeeds like nerve, so don't be afraid to try something new and different. Our President's Choice "Memories of . . ." sauces make child's play out of steering a course through the cuisines of the world. Bravado also comes in handy when you discover too late that the fire died for lack of briquets or gas, and you have to retreat to the kitchen or take everyone out for dinner.

Having said all that, remember the first rule for aspirants to the art of barbecue: Get organized. Then relax. Being prepared but flexible makes it easier to stay even-tempered in the face of events over which you have no control, such as the weather and the arrival time of guests, and still maintain your cool as the coals burn to a white hot ash.

OUR TOP THREE BARBECUE TIPS

Barbecuing is an inexact science and there are no hard-and-fast rules. So any book on the subject, including ours, will be very upfront in declaring: This is only a guide! Having said that, we unreservedly offer what we consider to be the top three barbecue tips.

   If you remember nothing else, remember to:

• Check your fuel supply. Whether you're using briquets or propane, you don't want to run out of fire before the meal is finished cooking.

• Always grease the grill before cooking and even during cooking if the food starts to stick. You can brush the grill with oil, rub it with an oiled cloth or use a vegetable cooking spray.

Caution: Use cooking spray only before lighting the fire; never spray into an open flame.

• Keep food moving on the grill. It promotes even cooking and prevents burning.

SOUPS &
STARTERS

PC Fresh Peeled Garlic

Did you ever wonder how chefs peel all that garlic? The short answer is, some of them don't. An Australian chef who trained at the famous Gleneagles Resort in Scotland put us onto the perfect PC product: ready-to-use peeled fresh garlic. It's ideal for lazy days and time-pressed cooks.

CHARRED TOMATO SOUP

Here are summer's best flavors, lightly charred and blended in one outstanding soup.

12	ripe tomatoes, halved and seeded	12
2	large yellow or red bell peppers	2
2	large Spanish onions, quartered	2
1	bulb fennel, quartered	1
1	zucchini, halved lengthwise	1
10	cloves PC Fresh Peeled Garlic, threaded on wooden skewer(s)	10
4 cups	chicken stock, homemade or made with PC Fresh Concentrated Chicken Stock	1 L
1 cup	PC La Elección del Presidente White Corn and Black Bean Salsa	250 mL
1 tbsp	PC Louisiana Hot Sauce	15 mL
	Salt and freshly ground pepper	
2 to 3 tbsp	PC Corn Oil	30 to 45 mL
4	PC Esplendido Corn Tortillas	4
	PC La Elección del Presidente Frozen Guacamole, thawed	

• On lightly greased grill over medium-high heat, grill tomatoes, peppers, onions, fennel, zucchini and garlic, turning periodically, until nicely charred. As each vegetable is finished cooking, remove from grill and let cool. Let peppers cool in sealed plastic bag.
• Remove skins from tomatoes and peppers. Coarsely chop tomatoes, peppers, onions, fennel and zucchini into 1/2-inch (1 cm) pieces. Finely chop garlic.
• Place chopped vegetables in large saucepan. Add chicken stock, salsa and hot sauce. Bring to boil over medium heat, then reduce heat and simmer for 10 minutes. Season with salt and pepper to taste.
• Meanwhile, in small skillet over medium-high heat, heat 1 tbsp (15 mL) corn oil. Cook tortillas one at a time, turning once, until crisp and golden, adding more oil as needed. Break each tortilla into quarters.
• Pour soup into bowls and stand 2 pieces of tortilla in each.
• Garnish with guacamole.
Makes 8 servings.

PC 'Too Good To Be True!'
Instant Spicy
Black Bean Soup

Traditional black bean soups start with a ritual soaking of beans followed by a few hours of simmering. In this quick-and-easy offering, we shave hours off the preparation time with our PC 'Too Good To Be True!' Instant Spicy Black Bean Soup. Start to finish, this dish takes 20 to 30 minutes to make — even less if you have all the ingredients assembled and prepare the soup while grilling the corn.

GRILLED CORN & BLACK BEAN SOUP

Black bean soup has been part of the Mexican diet for thousands of years, but there are few versions as appealing and simple to make as this one. What's more, if you forgo the nacho chips and sour cream garnishes, you can pretty much discount the very little fat this delicious dish contains.

If fresh corn is not available, substitute 1 1/2 cups (375 mL) of our PC Frozen Peaches & Cream Corn or PC Frozen Evensweeter White Corn. Simply allow corn to thaw, then stir-toss in a very hot cast-iron pan to impart a slightly charred flavor.

2	ears of corn, shucked	2
1	container (68 g) PC 'Too Good To Be True!' Instant Spicy Black Bean Soup	1
2 cups	boiling water	500 mL
1/2 cup	PC La Elección del Presidente Extra Chunky Mild Salsa Picante	125 mL
1/2 cup	PC Italian Magic Homestyle Italian Sauce	125 mL
1/4 cup	chopped fresh coriander	50 mL
	Juice of 1/2 lime	
	Salt	
	PC La Elección del Presidente Nacho Chips	
	Sour cream or PC 'Too Good To Be True!' Fat-Free Plain Yogurt	

• On lightly greased grill over medium-high heat, cook corn, turning periodically, until tender and lightly browned all over, about 8 to 10 minutes. Cut cobs in half. Then stand upright on cutting board and, using sharp knife, cut off kernels from top to bottom. Set aside.
• In medium-sized saucepan, mix together black bean soup, boiling water, salsa and Italian Magic. Bring to boil, reduce heat and let simmer for about 5 minutes. Stir in corn, coriander, lime juice and salt to taste.
• Garnish with nacho chips and sour cream or yogurt.
Makes 3 or 4 servings.

JUICES HITTING CHARCOAL OR LAVA ROCKS CREATE A SMOKY VAPOR THAT PERMEATES FOOD AND GIVES IT ITS CHARACTERISTIC BARBECUED FLAVOR.

PC Memories of Fuji
Shiitake Mushroom
Sauce

▲

PORTOBELLO CAPS CAN

MEASURE AN IMPRESSIVE

5 TO 6 INCHES

(12 TO 15 CM) IN

DIAMETER. SAVE THESE

FOR MARINATING —

ALWAYS GILL SIDE UP SO

THAT THE MARINADE

SEEPS INTO THE

MUSHROOM. YOU CAN

USE SMALLER

PORTOBELLOS FOR SOUP.

SINCE MUSHROOMS SOAK

UP WATER LIKE A

SPONGE, DON'T RINSE —

BRUSH CLEAN OR WIPE

WITH A DAMP

CLOTH, IF NECESSARY.

▼

Brown tableware, while perfectly acceptable in Germany or England, won't sell in France. Nor is cherry an acceptable color in the French medicine cabinet; *les français* much prefer purple *pilules* — preferably heart-shaped!

The experts unearthed these surprises when they surveyed 7,000 Europeans a few years ago. They also reported that 30% of the Britons they polled said Britain produces the best cheese (England is, after all, the home of Cheddar and Stilton). And 6% of them said Britain makes the best wine. Hail, Britannia!

Such chauvinistic fervor is not uncommon. The same poll showed that 85% of the Italians surveyed still live in the area where they were born. It's obviously not easy to say *arrivederci* to their superb regional gastronomy, or to such prized ingredients as the impressively large and flavorful mushroom called *portobello*.

Speak its name with reverence and be thankful that this prized species is now grown in Canada, thanks in large part to Hamilton, Ont., portobello enthusiast and our favorite mushroom grower, Lou Agro.

GRILLED PORTOBELLO MUSHROOM SOUP

The light, flavor-rich broth is intensified with PC Memories of Fuji Shiitake Mushroom Sauce.

1 lb	portobello mushrooms or mixed fresh mushrooms (e.g., portobello, oyster, shiitake)	500 g
1 tbsp	PC Chopped Garlic in Oil	15 mL
3 tbsp	PC Extra-Virgin Olive Oil	45 mL
	Juice of 1 lemon	
6 cups	boiling water	1.5 L
3 tbsp	PC Fresh Concentrated Beef Stock	45 mL
1/2 cup	PC Memories of Fuji Shiitake Mushroom Sauce	125 mL
	Salt and freshly ground pepper	
3 tbsp	chopped fresh parsley	45 mL

• Wipe mushrooms with damp cloth. Remove stems and reserve for other use.
• Mix together garlic, olive oil and lemon juice. Brush mushrooms all over with garlic mixture and let marinate, gill side up, for 10 to 20 minutes.
• Meanwhile, in medium saucepan, mix together boiling water and beef stock; let simmer for a few minutes. Stir in Memories of Fuji sauce; cover and continue simmering.
• Place mushrooms on grill over medium-high heat and cook about 6 to 8 minutes per side or until lightly charred. Thinly slice and add to broth; simmer 1 minute longer.
• Season with salt and pepper to taste. Sprinkle with parsley.
Makes 6 to 8 servings.

PC 'Too Good To Be True!'
20-Bean Soup

▲

THE NAME GAZPACHO

COMES FROM THE

ARABIC WORD MEANING

"SOAKED BREAD"

BECAUSE BREAD IS OFTEN

ADDED TO THICKEN

THE LIQUID. (THE ARABS

CONQUERED SPAIN IN

711 AD AND NAMED

THEIR SPANISH EMPIRE

"ANDALUZ.")

▼

The weight of tomato history belongs to Spain, even though Italy's Neapolitans claim that their ancestors were the first people brave enough to eat this New World fruit in the 16th century. Cortés escaped the first Aztec uprising in Mexico carrying seeds of the *xitomatl*, a fruit that Europeans long feared because it was related to the poisonous *deadly nightshade* plant.

Tomatoes are the foundation of Spanish *gazpacho*, a thirst-quenching soup from Andalusia which the Greeks and Romans regarded as "drinkable food."

Gazpacho is infinitely amenable to personal twists — indeed, every region of Spain has its own variations. Our version gets its tomato kick from PC La Elección del Presidente Extra Chunky Mild Salsa Picante and its substance from PC 'Too Good To Be True!' 20-Bean Soup.

20-BEAN GAZPACHO

This is a wonderfully thick gazpacho — yet light and refreshing. For variety, you can thin it by adding a little tomato or mixed vegetable juice. Serve it as a first course or light main dish with crusty bread and a glass of dry white wine.

1/2	seedless cucumber, peeled and coarsely chopped	1/2
1/2	red onion, coarsely chopped	1/2
1/2	red bell pepper, coarsely chopped	1/2
1 cup	chopped fresh coriander	250 mL
1 tbsp	PC Chopped Garlic in Oil	15 mL
1	jar (19 oz/540 mL) PC 'Too Good To Be True!' 20-Bean Soup	1
2 cups	PC La Elección del Presidente Extra-Chunky Mild Salsa Picante	500 mL
2 tbsp	fresh lemon juice	25 mL
	Salt and freshly ground pepper	
	PC San Francisco-Style Sourdough Croutons (optional)	

♦ In food processor or blender, combine cucumber, red onion, red pepper, coriander and garlic; lightly pulse until coarsely blended.
♦ Stir in bean soup and salsa.
♦ Add lemon juice and salt and pepper to taste. Chill well.
♦ If desired, garnish each serving with sourdough croutons.
Makes 4 to 6 servings.

Our flavorful
Corn Crab Cakes
with Spicy Rémoulade
Sauce conjure up
reminiscences of lazy
days at the beach.
Turn page for recipes.

PC Frozen Peaches
& Cream Corn

If you want fresh crabmeat, you'd better make neighbors with a crab. There are plenty of edible candidates — more than 4,000, in fact! One of the tiniest is the pea crab, which lives inside the shell of mussels; one of the Godzillas is Japan's deep-water giant crab, which has a span of 12$\frac{1}{2}$ feet (3.8 m). The robber crab wins points for upward mobility — it climbs palm trees and steals the coconuts (to make coconut cakes?)! Of course, among the most desirable is our Pacific Coast's own Dungeness crab, a delicacy that earns Vancouverites the envy of all other Canadians.

Crab is highly perishable, so even fresh crabmeat isn't really "fresh," unless you've picked it out of the shell yourself. What we the landbound generally buy is crabmeat that has been pasteurized at a temperature just high enough to kill most bacteria associated with spoilage. It still requires refrigeration, however. One of the best ways to enjoy crabmeat is in crab cakes.

CORN CRAB CAKES

These outstanding crab cakes are surprisingly simple to make — but use a gentle hand when forming the patties as the "batter" is quite moist. Chilling the mixture for 20 to 30 minutes makes it easier to handle.

Incidentally, it's fine to use surimi imitation crabmeat for these cakes, but check the label or consult the fishmonger as some brands may contain MSG.

$\frac{1}{4}$ cup	PC Unsalted Normandy-Style Cultured Butter	50 mL
$\frac{1}{2}$ cup	finely chopped onion	125 mL
$\frac{1}{2}$ cup	finely chopped celery	125 mL
1 cup	cornmeal	250 mL
$\frac{1}{2}$ cup	milk	125 mL
1 cup	PC Frozen Peaches & Cream Corn or PC Frozen Evensweeter White Corn	250 mL
12 oz	fresh or thawed frozen crabmeat, cartilage removed, or surimi imitation crabmeat	375 g
2 tbsp	PC Memories of Thailand Fiery Thai Dipping Sauce	25 mL
$\frac{1}{4}$ cup	finely chopped coriander	50 mL
	Spicy Rémoulade Sauce (recipe follows)	

◆ In medium-sized saucepan over medium-high heat, melt butter. Add onion and celery and cook, stirring, for 1 to 2 minutes until soft. Do not brown.

◆ Stir in $\frac{1}{2}$ cup (125 mL) cornmeal and reduce heat to medium. Continue cooking and stirring for another minute. Remove from heat and gradually add milk, stirring constantly. Let cool.

◆ Add frozen corn, crabmeat (if using thawed, drain well before using), Memories of Thailand sauce and coriander. Mix well. Cover and refrigerate for 20 to 30 minutes.

◆ Shape mixture into small patties, about 2 inches (5 cm) in diameter.

Carefully coat with remaining cornmeal and place on greased grill over medium heat for 3 to 4 minutes per side, or until firm to the touch and golden brown all over.

◆ Serve with Spicy Rémoulade Sauce.

Makes 12 cakes.

SPICY RÉMOULADE SAUCE

Pronounced RAY-moo-lahd, this French-inspired sauce is nothing more than tartar sauce with attitude. We've gone one step further by adding PC Memories of Thailand Fiery Thai Dipping Sauce.

PC The Ultimate Mayonnaise

1 cup	PC The Ultimate Mayonnaise	250 mL
1/2	red bell pepper, coarsely chopped	1/2
2	dill pickles, coarsely chopped	2
2 tbsp	chopped fresh chives	25 mL
1 tbsp	PC Dijon Mustard	15 mL
Dash	PC Louisiana Hot Sauce	Dash
Dash	PC 'Too Good To be True!' Light Worcestershire Sauce	Dash
1 tbsp	PC Memories of Thailand Fiery Thai Dipping Sauce	15 mL
3	green onions, chopped	3
	Juice of 1/2 lemon	
	Salt and freshly ground pepper	

◆ Place all ingredients in food processor or blender, adding salt and pepper to taste. Process just until blended.

◆ Taste and adjust seasoning.

◆ Chill until serving.

Makes 2 cups (500 mL).

*Life is so brief that we should not glance
either too far backwards or forwards. . .
therefore study how to fix our happiness
in our glass and on our plate.*

— Grimod de la Reynière

IF DESIRED, YOU CAN SUBSTITUTE PC MEMORIES OF BANGKOK SPICY THAI SAUCE FOR THE MEMORIES OF THAILAND FIERY THAI DIPPING SAUCE IN BOTH THE CRAB CAKES AND THE RÉMOULADE SAUCE.

PC La Elección del Presidente Extra Chunky Mild Salsa Picante

S alsa means "sauce" in Spanish, but it might as well mean "that which makes food worth eating." In Mexico and Southwestern households in the United States, where salsa has a permanent place at the table, it would be unthinkable to sit down to breakfast, lunch or dinner without one of these refreshing piquant sauces — even more shocking than if we had to forgo the salt, pepper and ketchup (don't tell the kids, but we sell more salsa in our stores than their favorite condiment)! Salsa can even turn into a spicy gazpacho (see recipe, page 24)!

NACHO PARTY DIP FOR A CROWD

This dip always gets rave reviews. And it's quick and easy to prepare with our instant black bean soup, which takes only minutes to rehydrate, and our frozen guacamole, which only needs thawing.

1 cup	boiling water	250 mL
1	container (68 g) PC 'Too Good To Be True!' Instant Spicy Black Bean Soup	1
1	container (340 g) PC La Elección del Presidente Frozen Guacamole, thawed	1
2 cups	PC La Elección del Presidente Extra Chunky Mild Salsa Picante	500 mL
2 cups	shredded mozzarella cheese	500 mL
2 cups	PC 'Too Good To Be True!' Low Fat Sour Cream Product	500 mL
1/2	can (398 mL) PC Super Colossal Pitted Black Olives, drained and coarsely chopped (about 7 olives)	1/2
1	red bell pepper, chopped	1
6 to 8	green onions, chopped	6 to 8
	PC La Elección del Presidente Nacho Chips or 'The Restaurant Blues' Blue Corn Tortilla Chips	

✦ Add boiling water to instant soup mix; stir well. Let stand 10 minutes.
✦ Spread soup along bottom of 10- or 11-inch (25 or 28 cm) square or round serving bowl. Spread guacamole over top. Spoon on salsa. Sprinkle with cheese.
✦ Spoon sour cream on top. Sprinkle with olives, red pepper and green onions.
✦ Refrigerate about 1 hour or longer until chilled.
✦ Serve with nacho or tortilla chips.
Makes 10 to 12 servings.

There's just something about a Mexican *quesadilla* (pronounced kay-sa-DEE-ya) that keeps us coming back for more. This simple grilled tortilla turnover, with a heart of melted cheese, can be eaten as an appetizer, a sandwich or a snack. The charm of a quesadilla is that you can enclose almost any ingredients you like, plain or fancy. More complicated turnovers, the ones filled and baked, are called *empanadas*.

Although quesadillas are usually a single tortilla folded over a filling and grilled, they can also be made by sandwiching the filling between two tortillas and then grilling this tortilla "stack."

PC Italian-Style Salsa

EGGPLANT QUESADILLAS

The jammy softness of the smoky flavored eggplant filling contrasts superbly with the papery thin crispness of the grilled tortilla. Make plenty as your friends will find these irresistible.

1	medium-size eggplant, peeled and cut lengthwise in ½-inch (1 cm) slices	1
2 to 3 tbsp	PC Roasted Garlic-Flavored Olive Oil Salt and freshly ground pepper	30 to 45 mL
3 tbsp	PC Italian-Style Salsa	45 mL
1 cup	grated Asiago cheese	250 mL
4	PC Esplendido Burrito-Size Flour Tortillas	4

• Brush eggplant slices all over with garlic-flavored olive oil; season with salt and pepper to taste.

• On lightly greased grill over medium-high heat, cook eggplant, turning frequently, until tender and lightly browned, about 5 to 7 minutes. Let cool and dice into ¼-inch (5 mm) pieces.

• In medium-sized bowl, mix together Italian-style salsa and grated Asiago cheese. Add chopped eggplant.

• Spoon half of eggplant mixture onto one of the tortillas, spreading evenly to edge. Top with another tortilla, pressing firmly to make a "sandwich." With remaining ingredients, prepare a second "sandwich."

• On greased grill over medium heat, cook quesadillas, turning often to avoid burning, until crisp and lightly browned on both sides. Let cool for about 30 seconds. Slice each into 6 to 8 wedges.

Makes 4 to 6 appetizer servings.

▲

THE SEEDS IN EGGPLANTS CAN MAKE THEM BITTER. SO WHEN SHOPPING, CHECK FOR GENDER. THE FEWEST SEEDS ARE IN THE MALE EGGPLANTS — THE ONES WITH THE SMOOTHEST STEM END. IN FEMALE EGGPLANTS, THE STEM END HAS A DEEP INDENTATION.

▼

PC Balsamic Vinegar

▲

FOR A CHANGE OF

PACE, YOU CAN

SUBSTITUTE ONE JAR

(350 mL) OF

PC RASPBERRY

BALSAMIC VINAIGRETTE

FOR THE DIJON

VINAIGRETTE IN THIS

RECIPE.

▼

In the most successful dishes, be they humble or luxurious, there's a perfect harmony between the sweet and sour elements. It's called the "acid balance." Acid balance keeps the palate awake. Introduce the elements of bitter and salt — the smokiness of charred vegetables and the seasoned edge of a smooth mustard — and you'll achieve a dish as close to perfection as a well-tuned Stradivarius.

GRILLED MIXED VEGETABLES WITH DIJON VINAIGRETTE

Vary the vegetable assortment according to taste and season. For a more pronounced flavor, marinate the vegetables overnight.

8 to 10	PC Jumbo Mushrooms for Stuffing or large white mushrooms	8 to 10
8 to 10	shiitake mushrooms	8 to 10
1	small zucchini	1
1	small eggplant	1
1	each red and yellow bell pepper	1
10 to 12	thin asparagus spears	10 to 12
1	red onion	1
12	cloves PC Fresh Peeled Garlic	12

Dijon Vinaigrette:

1/3 cup	PC Balsamic Vinegar	75 mL
1 tbsp	PC Dijon Mustard	15 mL
2	cloves PC Fresh Peeled Garlic, finely chopped	2
2 to 3 tbsp	chopped fresh coriander	30 to 45 mL
3/4 cup	PC Extra-Virgin Olive Oil	175 mL

◆ Slice jumbo and shiitake mushrooms into halves or quarters, depending on size. Cut zucchini and eggplant in half lengthwise, then cut into 1/4- to 1/2-inch (5 to 10 mm) slices.

◆ Cut red and yellow peppers in half. Remove seeds and cut each half into 4 strips. Trim coarse ends off asparagus, then blanch in boiling salted water for 30 seconds; drain. Slice top off onion and peel, keeping root end intact. Slice onion in half vertically through root. Cut each half into quarters, cutting through root so wedges hold together. Blanch garlic in salted boiling water for 4 minutes. Drain.

◆ Place vegetables in grill basket and grill over medium-high heat, turning periodically, for 15 to 20 minutes or until tender and lightly charred.

◆ Meanwhile, prepare Dijon Vinaigrette: Mix together vinegar, mustard, garlic and coriander. Gradually whisk in olive oil until thickened.

◆ Add enough vinaigrette to vegetables to coat. (Refrigerate any leftover vinaigrette for other use.) Toss lightly and serve at room temperature.

Makes 4 to 6 servings.

Garlic oil only *sounds* new. (It's mentioned in a 1934 cookbook called, with premature bravado, *The Twentieth Century Cook Book*.) But "roasted" garlic oil is another matter altogether. Roasting tames the pungency of garlic by caramelizing its natural sugars and allows the full resonance of garlic to shine through without the accompanying caustic heat.

We first applied the principle in our popular PC Memories of Gilroy Creamy Roasted Garlic Dressing. Recently, we used it to add an extraordinary rich garlic flavor to pure olive oil. It is a crucial ingredient in this recipe, which was developed by product developer and chef Ted Reader, our portobello pro and a master of the mushroom circuit.

PC Roasted Garlic-Flavored Olive Oil

GRILLED PORTOBELLO MUSHROOMS

Marinate the mushrooms early in the day so that they have time to soak up all the magnificent flavor of the balsamic vinegar and roasted garlic-flavored olive oil. During winter, you can cook the mushrooms in a shallow baking dish in a 400°F (200°C) oven for 15 to 20 minutes.

6 to 8	medium-size portobello mushrooms	6 to 8
1/2 cup	PC Balsamic Vinegar	125 mL
3 tbsp	chopped fresh coriander	45 mL
1 tbsp	coarsely ground pepper	15 mL
1 tsp	finely chopped garlic	5 mL
1 tsp	salt	5 mL
1 cup	PC Roasted Garlic-Flavored Olive Oil	250 mL

• Clean mushrooms with soft brush or damp cloth. Remove stems and reserve for other use.

• Prepare marinade: Mix together vinegar, coriander, pepper, garlic and salt. Gradually whisk in oil until mixture is thickened.

• Brush mushrooms all over with marinade, reserving extra marinade to use as a basting sauce. Arrange mushrooms gill-side up in shallow dish, cover loosely and let marinate in refrigerator for 4 to 6 hours.

• Place in grill basket or directly on grill over medium-high heat and cook 8 to 10 minutes per side or until tender, basting frequently with reserved marinade.

• Slice mushrooms but do not separate slices. Arrange on large platter or individual serving dishes.

Makes 6 to 8 servings.

TO GAIN "TEMPERATURE CONTROL" OVER A SIMPLE CHARCOAL BARBECUE, LET THE CHARCOAL BURN DOWN UNTIL IT'S GLOWING BENEATH A LAYER OF WHITE ASH — THE EQUIVALENT OF MEDIUM HEAT. THEN, INSTEAD OF SPREADING THE COALS EVENLY, HAVE FEWER COALS IN ABOUT ONE-THIRD THE COOKING AREA. THIS PROVIDES A COOLER SPOT WHERE YOU CAN MOVE FOOD THAT'S COOKING TOO QUICKLY.

▼

J ust when we thought we knew our Italian breads — *panini, crostini, bruschetta* — along comes *fettunta*.

Panini (pah-NEE-nee) is the name given to Italian sandwiches, although the word actually means "little breads." They're usually made with good, crusty, hearth-style bread, such as our PC Rustico Crusty Italian-Style White Bread.

Crostini (cros-TEE-nee) are small round toasts of about two or three bites, which makes them suitable for entertaining. They're usually cut from long, slender baguette-style loaves.

Bruschetta (bruce-KET-ta) is the original garlic bread, a rustic version brushed with oil, rubbed with garlic and roasted over the coals (*bruscare* means "to roast over coals"). Today it typically means grilled slices of crusty bread — we use either PC Rustico Crusty Italian-Style White Bread or our PC Splendido Italian-Style Flatbread — amply topped with whatever ingredients you choose, from chopped tomatoes and garlic to mashed beans and greens.

Fettunta (feh-TOON-ta) is, well, basically the same as the original bruschetta. A Tuscan specialty, it means "oiled slice."

PC Rustico Crusty Italian-Style White Bread

GOAT CHEESE BRUSCHETTA

Chop the tomatoes as close to serving time as possible so they don't lose too much liquid or flavor.

2 tbsp	PC Extra-Virgin Olive Oil	25 mL
1	onion, thinly sliced	1
1	clove PC Fresh Peeled Garlic, finely chopped	1
3	large ripe tomatoes, coarsely chopped	3
1/4 cup	chopped fresh basil	50 mL
1/2 cup	crumbled goat cheese	125 mL
	Salt and freshly ground pepper	
1	PC Rustico Crusty Italian-Style White Bread (280 g)	1
1/4 cup	PC Roasted Garlic-Flavored Olive Oil	50 mL

• In small skillet, heat olive oil. Add onion and cook for a few minutes until golden. Add garlic and cook 30 seconds longer or until fragrant. Turn off heat.

• Combine tomatoes, basil, goat cheese and onion mixture; mix well. Add salt and pepper to taste.

• Cut Rustico into slices, each about 1/2 inch (1 cm) thick. Brush all over with garlic-flavored oil and place on grill over medium-high heat for about 1 minute, turning once, until toasted and lightly charred around edges.

• Top grilled bread with a few spoonfuls of tomato mixture.

Makes 4 to 6 servings.

No sweet onion on hand? Here's how to mellow an ordinary yellow onion for salads or cooking: Chop and place in cold water for 15 to 20 minutes. The volatile oils that make it pungent will leach into the water. Drain well. (This is an old trick that Greek restaurants often use to make their country salad, or *HORIATIKI*, taste so great.)

These zesty chicken wing offerings are guaranteed to win you raves. Turn page for recipes.

PRIZEWINNING JAMAICAN-STYLE JERK CHICKEN WINGS

In 1991, we held an Insider's Report *barbecue contest and jerk wings came out on top. The recipe, which inspired a new "Memories of..." sauce, was created by Sharon and Joseph Mimran and their friends Michelle Lloyd-Berman and David Berman.*

1/2	bag (4 lb/1.8 kg) PC Gigantico Frozen Chicken Winglets and Wing Drumettes, thawed	1/2
3/4 cup	PC Memories of Montego Bay Jerk Marinade and Sauce or PC Vague Memories of Montego Bay Timid Jerk Marinade and Sauce	175 mL

♦ Place chicken wings in shallow glass dish. Add Memories of Montego Bay marinade and toss to coat. Cover and marinate in refrigerator for 4 to 6 hours or overnight. (Longer marinating produces spicier wings.)
♦ Arrange wings on baking sheet and place in 400°F (200°C) oven for 20 minutes. Transfer to grill basket and grill over medium heat, turning often, for 10 to 15 minutes or until crisp and brown.
Makes 4 to 6 servings.

ALLEN'S AMAZING MANHATTAN CHICKEN WINGS

One of our prized wing recipes comes from Toronto restaurateur John Maxwell, owner of Allen's (143 Danforth Ave.) and Orso (106 John St.).

1	bottle (270 mL) PC Gourmet Steak & Burger Sauce	1
2/3 cup	Worcestershire sauce	150 mL
1/4 cup	PC Louisiana Hot Sauce	50 mL
2 tbsp	PC Premium Alfalfa Honey	25 mL
1/2	bag (4 lb/1.8 kg) PC Gigantico Frozen Chicken Winglets and Wing Drumettes, thawed	1/2
3/4 cup	sour cream	175 mL
3/4 cup	PC The Ultimate Mayonnaise	175 mL
3/4 cup	crumbled Danish blue cheese	175 mL

♦ In large bowl, mix together steak sauce, Worcestershire sauce, Louisiana sauce and honey. Add wings and toss to coat. Cover and marinate in refrigerator for 2 to 4 hours.
♦ In small bowl, mix together sour cream, mayonnaise and blue cheese; cover and refrigerate until serving.
♦ Arrange wings on baking sheet (reserve leftover marinade for basting) and place in 400°F (200°C) oven for 20 minutes. Transfer to grill basket and grill

PC Gigantico Frozen
Chicken Winglets
and Wing Drumettes

▲

YOU CAN SUBSTITUTE
ONE BOX
(2.4 LB/1.1 KG)
OF PC FROZEN
SEASONED CHICKEN
WINGLETS AND WING
DRUMETTES, THAWED,
FOR THE 1/2 BAG
(4 LB/1.8 KG) OF
PC GIGANTICO FROZEN
CHICKEN WINGLETS AND
WING DRUMETTES
SPECIFIED IN
OUR WING RECIPES.

▼

over medium heat, turning and basting often, for 10 to 15 minutes or until glazed and crisp. Brush again with marinade just before removing from grill.
♦ Arrange wings on platter. Serve with blue cheese dip.
Makes 4 to 6 servings.

CHICKEN WINGS FOR A CROWD

These great-tasting wings are less spicy than the other wing recipes featured here — perfect for chicken wing lovers of all ages.

¹/₂ cup	PC Dry Garlic Sparerib Sauce	125 mL
¹/₂ tsp	PC Chopped Garlic in Oil	2 mL
¹/₂ cup	PC Tomato Ketchup	125 mL
¹/₂ cup	PC Plum Sauce	125 mL
¹/₂ cup	PC Hickory-Smoked Gourmet Barbecue Sauce	125 mL
1	bag (4 lb/1.8 kg) PC Gigantico Frozen Chicken Winglets and Wing Drumettes, thawed	1

♦ In large bowl, mix together garlic sparerib sauce, garlic, ketchup, plum sauce and barbecue sauce. Add wings and toss to coat. Cover and let marinate in refrigerator for 4 to 6 hours.
♦ Arrange wings on baking sheet (reserve leftover marinade for basting) and place in 400°F (200°C) oven for 20 minutes. Transfer to grill basket and grill over medium heat, turning and basting often, for 10 to 15 minutes or until crisp and brown.
Makes 8 to 10 servings.

Wow them with the appetizers: That's the first rule of entertaining in anyone's book. Just for starters, here are three sensational dips and our spicy roasted cashew nuts for nibbling. Pictured left to right: Charred Salsa, Roasted Cashew Nuts, Spicy Black Bean Dip and Guacamole with Charred Onions. For our quick-and-easy recipes, turn the page.

id you know: Tortilla "chips" evolved from triangles of corn tortillas that were grilled or deep-fried to crisp them up. Serve our fabulous dips with PC La Elección del Presidente Tortilla Chips, regular and blue corn, or PC La Elección del Presidente Nacho Chips, the original good-for-dipping round corn chip.

GUACAMOLE WITH CHARRED ONIONS

This delicious dip was test-launched at a housewarming for 50 people and everyone agreed that it was the best guacamole they'd ever tasted. The word "guacamole" comes via the Spanish from the Mexican Nahuatl word ahuacamolli, *or avocado sauce.*

1	red onion, sliced in 1/4-inch (5 mm) rounds	1
2 or 3	cloves PC Fresh Peeled Garlic	2 or 3
1	container (340 g) PC La Elección del Presidente Frozen Guacamole, thawed	1
1	ripe tomato, cut in cubes	1
4 tbsp	chopped fresh coriander	60 mL
	Juice of 1 lime	
	Salt and freshly ground pepper	

• Place onion and garlic in grill basket and grill over medium-high heat, turning occasionally, until tender and nicely charred.
• Chop onion and garlic and add to guacamole. Stir in tomato, coriander, lime juice and salt and pepper to taste. Chill until 30 minutes before serving.
• Just before serving, taste and adjust seasoning.
Makes about 2 cups (500 mL).

SPICY BLACK BEAN DIP

A great-tasting, low-fat dip — and it only takes a few minutes to make.

1	container (68 g) PC 'Too Good To Be True!' Instant Spicy Black Bean Soup	1
3/4 cup	boiling water	175 mL
1/2 cup	PC La Elección del Presidente Extra Chunky Salsa Picante, hot or mild	125 mL
1/2 cup	chopped fresh coriander	125 mL
	Salt	

• In small bowl, mix together black bean soup and boiling water. Let cool.
• Stir in salsa, coriander and salt to taste.
• Chill until 30 minutes before serving.
Makes 1 1/2 cups (375 mL).

▲

ROASTED
CASHEW NUTS
—•—

TOSS 1 LB (500 G)

TOASTED UNSALTED

CASHEWS WITH 1/3 CUP

(75 mL) PC MEMORIES

OF KOBE TAMARI GARLIC

MARINADE, 1 TSP

(5 mL) PC LOUISIANA

HOT SAUCE AND 2 TBSP

(25 mL) PC EXTRA-

VIRGIN OLIVE OIL.

MARINATE 1 HOUR.

ARRANGE ON BAKING

SHEET AND ROAST IN

350°F (180°C) OVEN

FOR 20 TO 30 MINUTES,

TURNING A FEW TIMES.

LET COOL.

MAKES 10 SERVINGS.

▼

CHARRED SALSA

This dip was inspired by the rich-flavored salsa that's served with deep-fried shrimp at Automatic Slim's Tonga Club in downtown Memphis.

6	plum tomatoes, quartered and seeded	6
2	red bell peppers, halved and seeded	2
1	red onion, sliced in ¼-inch (5 mm) rounds	1
2	cloves PC Fresh Peeled Garlic	2
2	jalapeño peppers, halved and seeded	2
2	ears of corn, shucked	2
2 cups	PC Italian Magic Homestyle Italian Sauce	500 mL
	Juice of ½ lemon	
	Salt and freshly ground pepper	
	PC Esplendido Fajita Size Flour Tortillas	

PC La Elección del Presidente Blue Corn Tortilla Chips

• Place tomatoes, red peppers, onion, garlic and jalapeño peppers in grill basket and grill over medium-high heat, turning occasionally, for 15 to 20 minutes or until tender and nicely charred. About halfway through cooking of vegetables, add corn to grill and cook, turning often, for about 5 to 10 minutes or until brown and crispy. Using sharp knife, cut kernels off cobs; set aside.

• Place grilled vegetables, except corn, in food processor. Quickly pulse on and off just until coarsely puréed. Stir in Italian Magic, lemon juice and salt and pepper to taste. Add corn. Chill until 30 minutes before serving.

• Just before serving, heat tortillas on grill for 30 to 60 seconds per side. Slice into pie-shaped wedges. Serve with salsa.

Makes 2½ cups (625 mL).

Close friends are folks who've sopped gravy out'n the same skillet.

— old range saying

Cowboy Steak 60

·

Chuckwagon Steak 61

·

Garlic Sirloin with Grilled Garlic 62

·

Beef Tenderloin with Blue Cheese Crust 64

·

Five Fabulous Burgers 66

·

Beef Ribs with Cowpoke Baked Beans 76

·

Beef Fajitas 78

·

Veal Chops with Mushroom Ragoût 80

BEEF &
VEAL

Fire & Smoke: The Story of Barbecue

It was the need to cook that taught man to use fire;
and it was by using that fire that man conquered Nature.

— Jean-Anthelme Brillat-Savarin

The Futurist magazine, looking as far as it dare into the future, says that come the year 2025, our lives will be a fusion of telecommunications and computers. "We'll *televote, teleshop, telework* and *tele-everything.* We'll *e-mail, tube* or *upload* letters to Mom. We'll go *MUDing* in cyberspace and mind our *netiquette* during virtual encounters." It's enough to bring on an attack of technoangst.

Say what they will, those with their gaze set forward; we envision that the best of the past will remain intact. And that includes backyard barbecuing.

Barbecue is a signpost to the awakening of taste, a marker sunk deep in the reaches of time when humankind first teased a flame into fire and started cooking dinner. No one knows who lit that first fire, but it was an achievement no less valuable to civilization than language. And no less startling than if Prometheus, a Titan among gods and friend of man, had indeed made his way up to heaven to steal a light at the chariot of the sun so that he might bring back the gift of fire, hidden in a stalk of fennel.

Like life itself, barbecue moves at its own pace. The Shilluks, a Sudanese tribe with a rich narrative tradition, hold a collective memory of what it was like when no one knew fire. Their dry, hot furnace of a land did the cooking for them. According to the respected elders who carry the tribal history in their heads, people used to set their food in the blazing sun. The parts exposed to this solar cooking (becoming more parched leather than char, we suspect) were divided among the men, while the women ate the cool, rare underneath. Sounds like an early steak *bleu* to us, only as yet there was no muddle of fries sharing the plate.

Before ovens, there was only the open flame. Fire pits have been found dating from 25,000 BC, and there's evidence of spit-roasting in the Ukraine from the 10th millenium BC — woolly mammoth tusks, strong enough to support an entire carcass, stuck points down on either side of a hearth. Food could be impaled or threaded on sticks and thrust into the fire; or tied, as in the case of large carcasses of meat or whole fish, to wooden lean-tos by a pit fire and left to cook.

No single culture can claim a monopoly on barbecue how-to. There are people all over the world, from the South Pacific islands to the hilltowns of Sardinia, from the Patagonian pampas of South America to the foothills of Alberta, who know plenty about cooking over glowing coals. Grill cuisine wouldn't be the same without the Greeks, the Italians, the Japanese, the Chinese, the Indonesians, the Mexicans, the Spanish, the Provençal French, the Cambodians, the Sri Lankans, the Koreans — now *there's* a people who know their barbecue: *Bulgogi* is the name they give to spicy strips of grilled beef with side dishes that can be downright incendiary. It's as if having tamed the flame, man sought out heat as a flavor itself.

Even an old boot tastes good if it is cooked over charcoal.

— old Italian saying

Most food historians accept that the word *barbecue* — as opposed to the method — derives from the Arawak word for a three-legged frame, *barbacoa,* that conquistadors saw the Taino and Arawak Indians of Haiti and Guyana place over pits in the ground for smoking fish or cooking pork. These trivets were called *boucans* and the cooking technique, to *boucan.* With a twist of the word, the cook became a *buccaneer.* Barbecue is one of the buccaneer's gifts to the culinary arts as these pirates learned to boucan as expertly as the natives. For their part, the Caribbean Indians may have borrowed the idea from South American Indians. The Spaniards adapted the method, using frameworks of sticks set on posts to roast large animals, and settlers to the New World continued the practice to prepare their fish, pigs and sheep.

Less credence is given to the notion that barbecue derives from the French *barbe à queue,* or "from beard to tail," which describes spit-roasting a whole cow or pig over a slow fire. The Greeks taught spit-roasting to the Etruscans, the ancient people who lived in the region that is now Tuscany in Italy. They subsisted on a diet of spit-roasted meat and fish, fresh vegetables, bread and fruit. Quite happily, from all reports; but then, why not? Modern-day Tuscans continue to eat all manner of food cooked over smoldering fires flavored with such fragrant wood as pine or juniper. "In the *trattorie*," notes British food writer Valentina Harris, "you'll see customers watching with great care their half chicken or steak cooking on the scented fire, and it's they who decide when the meal is ready."

The Etruscans passed along the art of spit-roasting to the Romans, who in turn introduced the method to England in 42 AD. By medieval times, grand edifices of spits were being erected in front of huge fireplaces in the homes of the wealthy all over England, giving rise to the job of spit-boy — and later in France, to meat chef, or *rôtisseur*.

The modern-day rotisserie is one of those everyday contrivances that keeps us connected to our brothers and sisters from the past. The medieval Chinese were hot on grilled chicken — our domestic chicken descended from the red jungle fowl that still lives in southeast Asia — as were the French of that day. On the rue de la Huchette, in Paris, spits turned non-stop and braziers burned continuously to feed the voracious appetite for poultry of all kind, the flames of the fires being smothered only for the penitential fasting of Lent.

Grilled fish. Pit-cooked meat. Spit-cooked chicken. We cling stubbornly to simple foods simply prepared. The unassailable reason why is that they taste so good! To this day we haven't lost our taste for a small hot bird and a large cold drink. Even a burnished leaf of radicchio transferred from grill to plate becomes a valued culinary artifact.

Hot and sweet and red and greasy,
I could eat a gallon easy:
Barbecue sauce! Lay it on, hoss.
Nothing is dross under barbecue sauce.

— Roy Blount Jr.

To the everlasting good fortune of us all, almost any food you can think of seems to taste better when it's grilled. Even a stick of bologna — scored, cooked till it sizzles and brushed with barbecue sauce for a shiny finish — is worthy food for a feast. Foods set a tone of their own, and there's no more convivial fare than what comes off a grill. Barbecued beef, barbecued lamb, barbecued ribs, goat, ham or chicken . . . even the ubiquitous but essential barbecued burger, so fast and convenient at a backyard barbecue.

If you're feeling really lazy, you don't have to "do" much of anything with foods earmarked for the grill. Just cook and let one of our many President's Choice sauces stave off ennui. Or not. Subjecting food to the aromatic smoke of a fire makes the flavor fundamentalist happy. Seasonings and marinades enhance the flavor, but purists are content with smoke alone. They prefer to bathe their meat in the warm haze that represents the energy of fire rather than the fire itself. At the other end of the scale are those who pound, shred and drown food in sauce. But hey, that's barbecue too. Barbecue began as a rite of survival. Adaptability is its middle name.

Knowing which foods to grill is easy if you keep in mind that grilling and sautéeing call for similar cuts of meat. Any lean meat is suitable for fast cooking. Steaks or chops are ideal candidates, as are paillards, thinly cut portions of lean beef or poultry that are pounded flat for even cooking. The more tough connective tissue contained in the meat, the lower the heat and the slower the cooking. Pork butt and brisket are prime examples.

Timing in barbecuing is a learned skill. Grilling is faster than slow cooking, which can take 2 to 24 hours — and you must check in from time to time. But grilling still takes as long as it takes!

*The smell of roasting meat together with that of burning
fruitwood and dried herbs, as voluptuous as incense in a church,
is enough to turn anyone into a budding gastronome.*

— Claudia Roden

Barbecue is not only the way food was first cooked after the discovery of fire — it's also ritual cooking at its best. And meat is part of the ritual. Many people think only of meat as they light the grill and enter into barbecue territory. Red meat, that is. Not white meat. And not that "cold, bloodless meat" — aka fish — that used to replace meat at Lent in respectful denunciation of such earthly appetites as the passion for food.

The procurement of meat has always been cause for celebration. Prometheus not only stole fire from the gods but he was also the first to keep animals. Until his gift of food and fire, man relied on the success of the hunt. In Rio Grande do Sul, the centre of Brazil's cattle country, a celebratory rite is the *churrasco a gaucha*, or cattleman's barbecue. In the early days, this would have consisted of freshly killed beef cooked over an open pit fire. Today, a *churrasco* is the arena of the specialist. Beef, chicken, pork, lamb and sausages are cooked on skewers plunged firmly into the ground beside the pit fire, and the meats, centred over the heat, are left to cook until meltingly tender, with an occasional swabbing of garlicky brine.

"Beef and Liberty" was the motto of The Sublime Society of Beef Steaks founded in 1737 in England. This London club endured for 130 years and counted among its members the Earl of Sandwich and King George IV, although George was forced to wait for a vacancy among the 24 spots before gaining admittance to this convivial gathering. Members' buttons and rings were impressed with a gridiron and the club motto, and at each meeting, a butcher was sent along with the meat to cut it and to take back what was not eaten. In the waning years of the club, one butcher, exasperated with humoring so many whims — "A thick steak!" "A thin steak!" "An underdone steak!" — and seeing how the general appetite for meat had become a travesty of what it once was (the poor man was taking back more than members were eating!), upped and quit, which helped speed the club's demise.

Meat hunger rises and falls. From the ashes of that Sublime Society rose a new club in Quebec City, which modelled its chapter after the London namesake. Elsewhere in the New World, the issue was one of getting enough meat. The early French settlers brought in their own domesticated cows to begin populating the St. Lawrence Valley. The West ultimately benefited from the Spanish colonies on the Caribbean islands, where the first ranches were established. That cattle frontier slowly pushed its way northward into Mexico, then into the United States and finally up to Canada, with scrawny longhorns being replaced over time by meatier Herefords and the stocky Black Angus. Meat came to symbolize plenty. In the late 1800s, a dime could buy plenty of steak — enough to feed half a dozen people.

Across the southern United States and all across the Pacific, however, pork — not beef — is the meat dedicated to barbecue. Pork is what the Arawaks liked best to boucan. And pork is easier to confront than a bear, which Canadian colonists reported tastes remarkably similar. If the world stopped raising pork, legions of barbecuers would untie their apron strings and lay down their tongs forever. Many would hail from those parts of the world where pork shoulder, ribs and sausage are the soul of charcooking, but a lot of them would be your friends and neighbors in cities and towns across Canada. A plump pig has always been part of the country diet, since pork is easy to raise and almost entirely edible.

By now you might be wondering whether barbecue can exist without meat. The answer is, of course! "Meat" didn't always mean animal; about 600 years ago, the word signified any nourishment. Vegetables are always a welcome change from too much hoof and horn. If vegetables are your meat, you can assemble a terrific menu by drawing from our appetizers and side dishes — for example, Eggplant Quesadillas (p. 33), Grilled Polenta with Caramelized Onions and Gorgonzola (p. 190), Grilled Endive and Radicchio with Tuscan-Style Beans (p. 192), Grilled Potatoes with Garlic Aïoli (p. 214), Grilled Bread Salad with Roasted Red Peppers and Cherry Tomatoes (p. 220) and Sweet Pea Salad (p. 224). For more ideas, check the index.

Pickin' up bones to keep from starvin'.
Pickin' up chips to keep from freezin'.
Pickin' up courage to keep from leavin'.
Way out West in no-man's land.

— sign on a wagon

For those of us who love to barbecue, the grill pit is our place of worship and our instruments of ritual are the long-handled fork and spatula. In our heads and on our bookshelves, we carry the sacred scriptures — i.e., our favorite barbecue recipes — despite the cruel irony that grilling is, by nature, exasperatingly inexact. Knowledge is gained by trial and error. Even fuel, as a rule, is whatever is at hand. In some parts of Spain today, food is cooked over fires fueled with ground walnut shells and pulverized olive pits.

Dedicated barbecuers loath to part with their hard-won secrets would have us believe they carry out their ritual responsibility with ashes blowing in their face from an open pit fire. But there's rarely any evidence of that. Flying sparks from hardwood — the major, if not the *only* fuel for many thousands of years — might be expected if you're cooking *al carbón* in Spain or northern Mexico, or in the hilltowns of Greece or Italy, or in any of the backyard kettle grills across Canada that are still taking their lumps today. More likely, the grill your barbecue buddy is using is gas-fueled, and it maintains its heat well enough without any interference from the cook.

Over the years, any number of materials have been used to keep the fires going. The Scythians of 6th century BC used the fatty bones of the beasts they hunted to fuel the fires over which they cooked them. Of course, we prefer to think of the Scythians' heirs, the Mongols, as the original brazier men, owing to their purported ingenuity on the trail. We last saw them using their helmets to charcook their food over blazing pinecones and twigs. At their permanent camps, their braziers burned over fires of thorns, wormwood roots and cattle dung.

But let's leave those ghostly hordes of barbecue barbarians, at times numbering as many as 100,000, to thunder across the barren steppes of Asia for eternity, "the neighing of their steeds . . . enough to make Heaven shut its ears and their arrows convert the sky to a sea of reeds." For the real action in barbecue, and where we find the great leap that turned barbecue into the social shrine it is today, we need to go back to the future to which we have already alluded.

Back to the New World. Here we'll find a fraternity of the good and courageous, as well as armed desperadoes, rustlers and ne'er-do-wells — the rovers on horseback who opened up the mountains and the plains and drove cattle to market, or at least from one place to another for better grazing, as herdsmen have done for millennia. They're early incarnations of the venerated North American "cowboy," even though the word, as we know it today, didn't exist until about 1865; and then, it was only used snidely to describe drifters and cattle thieves. Before wearing the cowboy hat, cattle ranchers were called buckaroos, a corruption of the Spanish *vaquero* for cowherd. The vaqueros, many of whom were of Indian or African ancestry and valued for their knowledge of herding techniques, were the first to use horses and ropes to tend cattle.

Perhaps these early cowboys in the arid Southwest had the best of all choices for barbecuing: mesquite (mess-KEET). Mesquite is a weed tree that burns extremely hot, which makes it ideal for grilling. It also kicks up a lot of smoke unless transformed into charcoal, which burns cleaner and hotter. The charcoal is formed when the wood is left to smolder without oxygen until completely blackened. (An airtight covering of clay and straw does the job nicely.)

We modern-day practitioners of the ancient art of barbecue must still gather fuel for the event, although now we can hop in the car and drive to the supermarket or visit the nearest propane refill centre. As ever, the best advice is to use what's economical and available, and what you're psychologically equipped to handle. Mesquite charcoal burns so fiercely that it can melt your grate if you don't pay attention! Hardwood charcoal briquets or natural lump charcoal are readily available. Wood is good, too, if you have access to a few cords of maple, hickory, oak, pecan, dogwood, beech, birch or ash — they're all top-notch, and chips from any of them can add flavor to your food.

Many modern barbecuers, however, pledge their allegiance to the gas grill, secure in its push-button convenience and comforted by the knowledge that they can readily indulge their yen for barbecue the minute it strikes.

Some dishes are "all hat and no cowboy" — they look impressive but leave you hungry. Our sizzling Cowboy Steak isn't one of them.

PC Memories of Kobe
"The 2 Minute Miracle"
Tamari Garlic Marinade

TO GIVE STEAKS A
PROFESSIONAL CHEF'S
"CROSS-CHAR"
MARKINGS, ROTATE
THEM A QUARTER-TURN
ON THE GRILL
HALFWAY THROUGH
COOKING
ON EACH SIDE.

Italy has its spaghetti westerns but it also has a long-time beef tradition (*Italia* means land of cattle). There, you can order an inch-thick (2.5 cm) grilled steak that stretches before you like a never-ending horizon. Too big for its plate, the famous *bistecca alla fiorentina* can weigh 3 pounds (1.5 kg).

On this side of the Atlantic, nothing beats a thick rib steak with a bone left on for gripping or gnawing when you have a mean appetite for meat. (Forget for a moment that true cowboys, the kind depicted in dime-store westerns, preferred to eat very thinly sliced steaks because the meat was usually tough.) We're talking "in your face" barbecue. And this recipe proves you don't have to drown meat in marinade to give it flavor. That's the wonder of PC Memories of Kobe.

COWBOY STEAK

Ask your butcher for 2-inch-thick (5 cm) rib steaks, then have him french them — or french them yourself at home. "Frenched" is the term butchers use when they scrape away the meat to expose the top 2 to 3 inches (5 to 7.5 cm) of bone.

Serve this sensational steak with grilled sweet corn, roasted garlic, field tomatoes and baby new potatoes tossed with chopped fresh herbs and a little butter.

2	bone-in rib steaks, each about 16 to 24 oz (500 to 750 g) and 2 inches (5 cm) thick, preferably frenched	2
2 tbsp	finely chopped PC Fresh Peeled Garlic	30 mL
1 tbsp	chopped fresh rosemary	15 mL
1 tbsp	coarsely ground pepper	15 mL
1/2 cup	PC Memories of Kobe "The 2 Minute Miracle" Tamari Garlic Marinade	125 mL

• Wipe beef with damp cloth and pat dry.
• Mix together garlic, rosemary and pepper.
• Rub steaks all over with garlic-rosemary mixture. Then brush with Memories of Kobe sauce. Let marinate for 20 to 30 minutes.
• On lightly greased grill over medium-high heat, cook steaks for 8 to 10 minutes per side for medium rare or to desired doneness.
• Let meat rest for 5 minutes. Slice and serve.
Makes 4 servings.

Chuck means many things to many people. To anyone who owns a power drill, it's the T-shaped piece used to tighten the drill bit. Among ranch hands, it's slang for food.

Sometimes it connotes hamburger meat, since ground-up chuck — a beef cut that contains parts of the shoulder blade — produces delicious results in a beef patty. This same cut produces steaks that demand a little more care if they're to come out tender, but their flavor is certainly worth it. For instance, a cross rib steak cut from the chuck is an excellent economy cut for barbecue season, and it can yield tender and moist eating, provided it is first marinated overnight and then braised slowly.

CHUCKWAGON STEAK

The flavorful marinade in this recipe was inspired by the delicious braising sauce used for Chuckwagon Pot Roast in our first President's Choice cookbook.

1 cup	PC Tournament Barbecue Sauce	250 mL
2 tbsp	PC Herb & Pepper Spicy Olive Oil	25 mL
1 to 2 tbsp	PC 'Too Good To Be True!' Light Worcestershire Sauce	15 to 30 mL
1/2 tsp	dry mustard	2 mL
2 to 3 tbsp	fresh lemon juice	30 to 45 mL
1 tbsp	coarsely cracked pepper	15 mL
	Salt	
2 lb	cross rib steak cut from the chuck, about 1 1/2 inches (4 cm) thick	1 kg

• In shallow glass pan, mix together barbecue sauce, olive oil, Worcestershire sauce, mustard, lemon juice, pepper and salt to taste.
• Place steak in marinade and turn to coat well. Cover and marinate in refrigerator for 6 to 8 hours or, preferably, overnight. Reserve marinade.
• On lightly greased grill over medium-high heat, cook steak with lid down for 10 to 15 minutes per side or until desired doneness, basting occasionally with reserved marinade. Cut into thin slices and serve.

Makes 4 to 6 servings.

PC Dry Garlic
Sparerib Sauce

The Unofficial Official Grill Chef's Hand Test is a simple and efficient way to determine whether it's time to throw on the steaks. To tell when the coals are ready, hold your hand about 4 inches (10 cm) above the cooking surface and see how long you can keep it there. For low heat, expect 5 seconds; medium high, 3 to 4 seconds; and for high, about 2 seconds.

GRILLED GARLIC SIRLOIN

We tried this succulent steak with and without PC Memories of Kobe and everyone preferred the subtle but welcome presence of our tamari garlic marinade.

1 cup	PC Dry Garlic Sparerib Sauce	250 mL
1 tbsp	PC Memories of Kobe "The 2 Minute Miracle" Tamari Garlic Marinade	15 mL
4	cloves PC Fresh Peeled Garlic, chopped	4
1 tbsp	freshly ground pepper	15 mL
4	PC Baron of Beef Top Sirloin Steaks	4

♦ In shallow glass dish, mix together garlic sparerib sauce, Memories of Kobe sauce, chopped garlic and pepper. Add steaks and turn once or twice to coat well. Cover and marinate in refrigerator for 4 to 6 hours. Let meat return to room temperature before cooking.

♦ Place steaks on lightly greased grill over high heat and cook for 3 to 5 minutes per side or to desired doneness.

Makes 4 servings.

GRILLED SKEWERED GARLIC

To prevent burning, soak wooden skewers in water for at least 30 minutes before using.

2 tbsp	PC Roasted Garlic-Flavored Olive Oil	25 mL
1 tbsp	PC Balsamic Vinegar	15 mL
	Salt and freshly ground pepper	
25	cloves PC Fresh Peeled Garlic, gently boiled in water to cover for 3 minutes and drained	25

♦ In small bowl, combine oil, vinegar and salt and pepper to taste. Add garlic and toss to coat.

♦ Thread garlic onto single or double skewers, reserving oil-vinegar mixture in bowl. Place on grill over medium heat and cook for about 6 to 8 minutes or until golden brown, turning and basting often with reserved oil-vinegar mixture. Serve as a side dish or appetizer.

Makes 4 to 6 servings.

PC Italian-Style
Breadcrumbs

To prevent meat from drying out in the refrigerator, coat lightly with vegetable oil. Some noted chefs even salt their meat very, very lightly, saying that this enables the seasoning to penetrate the meat and thus reduce the amount needed during grilling.

▼

When product developer Ted Reader, a skilled chef in his own right, came back from Chicago last year, he was rarin' to make a dish he'd tried at a tapas restaurant called Cafe Ba-Ba-Reeba. The dish was called *Solomillo con Cabrales*, or grilled beef tenderloin with blue cheese crust.

It sounded intriguing and what Ted recreated in the kitchen tasted extraordinary. The tenderloin was succulent and buttery smooth, and it bore an attractive pale crust, as fork tender as the beef and redolent of blue cheese and herbs. It was the perfect marriage of flavors. Here's Ted's recipe.

GRILLED BEEF TENDERLOIN WITH BLUE CHEESE CRUST

The aromatic topping is very easy to handle and can be made ahead; shaped into patties that are placed on the steaks, the mixture cooks to form an even crust over the meat.

2 to 3 lb	beef tenderloin, cut in 8 steaks	1 to 1.5 kg
3 tbsp	PC Roasted Garlic-Flavored Olive Oil	45 mL
2 tbsp	PC Aged Red Wine Vinegar	30 mL
	Freshly ground pepper	
1 cup	crumbled blue cheese	250 mL
1 tbsp	chopped fresh thyme or 1 tsp (5 mL) dried	15 mL
1 tbsp	chopped fresh rosemary or 1 tsp (5 mL) dried	15 mL
1/4 cup	chopped onion	50 mL
1 tbsp	chopped PC Fresh Peeled Garlic	15 mL
1/2 cup	PC Italian-Style Breadcrumbs	125 mL
2 tbsp	water	25 mL
	Salt	

• Wipe meat with damp cloth and pat dry.
• Mix together oil, vinegar and freshly ground pepper to taste. Brush all over steaks. Cover and let marinate in refrigerator for 2 hours, turning occasionally. Let return to room temperature while preparing blue cheese crust.
• In food processor, combine blue cheese, thyme, rosemary, onion, garlic, breadcrumbs, water and salt and pepper to taste. Process until mixture forms a thick paste. Shape into 8 small patties.
• On greased grill over medium-high heat, grill beef for about 3 to 4 minutes; turn and place a blue cheese patty on top of each steak. Using spatula, pat down cheese patty to flatten and form crust over beef.
• Continue cooking for a few minutes until beef is cooked to desired doneness and cheese mixture is melted.
Makes 8 servings.

PC Memories of Kobe
Frozen Thick &
Juicy Beef Burgers

*Let the stoics
say what they
please, we do not
eat for the good
of living, but
because the meat
is savory and
the appetite is keen.*

— R.W. Emerson
(1803-82)

Hey — it's summer! Anything goes. Even this eye-popping Super Colossal Kobe Burger Stack made with President's Choice Memories of Kobe Thick & Juicy Beef Burgers. For cantilevered jaws only. For more burger ideas, turn the page.

SUPER COLOSSAL KOBE BURGER STACK

This may only be one "burger," but feel free to scale down according to the size of your appetite and depth of your burger deficiency.

3	PC Memories of Kobe Frozen Thick & Juicy Beef Burgers, unthawed	3
2	rings red bell pepper	2
2	rings yellow bell pepper	2
2	rings orange bell pepper	2
2	slices red onion	2
1	large slice ripe tomato	1
1	kaiser bun or other crusty roll	1
	PC Extra-Virgin Olive Oil	
1	lettuce leaf	1
1	dill pickle, halved lengthwise	1
1	slice PC 4-year-old White Cheddar Cheese	1

• On greased grill over medium-high heat, cook Memories of Kobe burgers for 3 to 5 minutes per side or to desired doneness. While burgers are cooking, add red, yellow and orange peppers to grill along with onion slices and tomato. Cook vegetables about 1½ to 2 minutes per side or until lightly charred.

• Cut kaiser bun in half and brush each half with oil. Place cut-side down on grill and toast for 1 to 2 minutes.

• To assemble burger, arrange bottom half of bun on plate, then layer as follows: lettuce, tomato, burger, dill pickle, red peppers, burger, onions, yellow peppers, burger, cheese, orange peppers and top of bun.

Makes 1 super colossal burger.

These four sumptuous burgers are all big on flavor (some are equally big in size)! Pictured from left: Our wicked One Pounder with Vidalia Onion Rings, Double-Decker Cheeseburger, Nacho Burger and Havarti Burger.
See next page for recipes.

HAVARTI BURGERS

MIX TOGETHER 1 LB
(500 G) GROUND BEEF
AND 1 TSP (5 mL)
PC MEMORIES OF KOBE
TAMARI GARLIC
MARINADE. SHAPE INTO
4 BALLS. COMBINE
1/2 CUP (125 mL)
GRATED HAVARTI
CHEESE AND
1 TBSP (15 mL)
PC RUSSIAN-STYLE
SWEET MUSTARD. MAKE
WELL IN BURGERS AND
FILL WITH CHEESE
MIXTURE. RESHAPE BALLS
SO CHEESE IS ENTIRELY
ENCASED IN BEEF.
FLATTEN INTO PATTIES.
GRILL 5 MINUTES PER
SIDE OR TO DESIRED
DONENESS. SERVE WITH
LETTUCE, TOMATO AND
ONION SLICES ON GRILLED
WEDGES OF PC RUSTICO
CRUSTY ITALIAN-STYLE
WHITE BREAD.
MAKES 4 SERVINGS.

NACHO BURGERS

The secret ingredient in these sensational burgers is the crushed tortilla chips, which lend both flavor and texture. A food processor grinds them most efficiently.

1 lb	medium ground beef	500 g
1 cup	PC La Elección del Presidente Extra-Chunky Salsa Picante, hot or mild	250 mL
2 tbsp	chopped fresh coriander	25 mL
1 tbsp	PC Louisiana Hot Sauce	15 mL
2 tsp	PC Key West Lime Juice	10 mL
1/2 tsp	chili powder	2 mL
1/2 tsp	ground cumin	2 mL
1/2 cup	finely ground PC La Elección del Presidente Nacho Chips (about 15 chips)	125 mL
	Salt and freshly ground pepper	
4	sesame egg buns or kaiser buns	4
1/2 cup	shredded Monterey Jack cheese	125 mL
1/2 cup	PC La Elección del Presidente Frozen Guacamole, thawed	125 mL

♦ Mix together beef, 1/2 cup (250 mL) salsa, coriander, Louisiana hot sauce, lime juice, chili powder, cumin, nacho chips and salt and pepper to taste.
♦ Shape into patties and place on lightly greased grill over medium-high heat. Cook for 4 to 5 minutes per side or to desired doneness. Shortly before burgers are finished cooking, place buns on grill and toast lightly.
♦ Place bottom halves of buns on individual plates. Top each with a burger, shredded cheese, guacamole and salsa. Place tops of buns next to burgers. **Makes 4 servings.**

DOUBLE-DECKER CHEESEBURGER WITH BACON, LETTUCE & TOMATO

On Oct. 12, 1934, Carl Kaelin asked his wife "to lay a piece of cheese on those burgers" at the Kentucky family restaurant and the cheeseburger was born. (Or so the story goes.)

8	PC Tournament Frozen Thick and Juicy Beef Burgers, unthawed	8
4	slices PC 4-year-old White Cheddar Cheese	4
4	large kaiser buns or other crusty buns, cut in half	4
4	each lettuce leaves and tomato slices	4

12	slices PC Naturally Smoked Bacon,
	cooked until crisp and drained
	PC Dijon or PC Brown and Spicy Mustard
	PC Tomato Ketchup or PC La Elección del Presidente
	Salsa Ketchup Sauce

- On lightly greased grill over high heat, cook frozen burgers for 4 to 5 minutes per side for medium or to desired doneness. About 1 or 2 minutes before burgers are finished cooking, top half of them with cheese. Place kaiser buns on grill and heat for 1 minute until lightly toasted.
- To assemble, place bun bottoms on plates. Layer each with lettuce, plain burger, cheese-topped burger, tomato and 3 strips of bacon. Add top of bun and serve with mustard and ketchup.

Makes 4 servings.

PC Tournament
Frozen Thick and Juicy
Beef Burgers

ONE POUNDER
WITH VIDALIA ONION RINGS

In our efforts to develop the ultimate bigger burger, we tested 8-, 10-, 12- and 16-ouncers. Each time, the one-pounders cooked up juicier and more flavorful than the others. Look for this truly awesome burger among PC frozen boxed meats — it's the one shaped like a porterhouse steak.

2	large Vidalia onions, cut in ¹/4-inch (5 mm) rings	2
cups	milk	500 mL
cups	all-purpose flour	500 mL
2	PC "The One Pounder" Steakhouse-Style Frozen	2
	Beef Burgers, thawed	
	PC Peanut Oil for frying	
	Salt and freshly ground pepper	

- Soak onions in milk for 30 minutes. Drain well, reserving milk. Toss onions in flour and then return to milk. Drain again and toss a second time in flour. Set aside.
- On lightly greased grill over medium-high heat, cook burgers 8 to 10 minutes per side for medium.
- Pour oil into heavy medium-sized saucepan to a depth of 2 inches (5 cm). Heat to a temperature of 375°F (190°C). Add onions in small batches and cook just until golden brown, about 2 to 3 minutes. Drain on paper towels. Season with salt and pepper to taste.
- Arrange burgers on plates. Top each with a mountain of onion rings.

WHEN FORMING HAMBURGER PATTIES, NEVER OVERHANDLE THE MEAT OR BURGERS WILL BE TOO COMPACT. SHAPE PATTIES QUICKLY AND WITH A LIGHT HAND. YOUR BURGERS WILL TASTE BETTER FOR IT.

The steak is bloody so you send it back. Then the chef calls the police. What next?

A SYDNEY couple visit a Balmain restaurant for

Enough, cries the chef, who will not cook anymore. Conflict

Thursday 1 ...ruary 1994   A–9

— headline in Melbourne newspaper, *The Age*, Feb. 17, 1994

A CAUTIONARY TALE

R ose pink and warm. Crusted, cool and red. Charred black and beige. People want their meat the way they want it. So don't take it personally when they don't appreciate *their* meat *your* way. To impress upon you the uselessness of expending emotional energy and material resources trying to convert others to your way of thinking, we pass along this cautionary tale, sent to us by one of our product developers, Chris Grikscheit, when he was in Australia. It's the story of a diplomatic disaster at a Sydney restaurant.

The cast of this *mise en scène* includes one disgruntled customer who kept sending her steak back to the kitchen to eliminate all traces of red (and then started in on the pink, it being Valentine's Day not weighing heavily in her considerations); an unrepentant chef who unequivocally refused to cook the bejesus out of it; and the police who answered the chef's call when the customer refused to pay the $13.50 tab for the steak. In short, it was not a traditional romantic dinner for two. "I'm out with my loved one and they're calling the police over a steak," said the aggrieved young woman.

There was no consensus around town as to who deserved a comeuppance. The situation clearly revolved around moral issues, which are never black and white but more like grey — which, as it happens, is exactly the color the restaurant patron wanted her steak to be. In steak matters, however, grey is open to interpretation. Said the chef, "As far as I'm concerned, the product went out as ordered. It was almost bereft of blood with the tiniest bit of pink in the meat."

Some cheered the chef for digging in his heels and refusing to subject his top-quality, grain-fed beefsteak to further abuse. Exclaimed one sympathetic restaurateur: "I wouldn't tell an artist how to paint a picture!" Others jeered his arrogance, though not even they applauded the woman's taste in meat. The customer was paying, so she had every right to refuse to pay for meat that wasn't cooked to her liking. "We are professionals there to please our customers — not teach them," commented the local oracle on all grill matters.

The moral of this tale: You need not applaud other people's taste in food, but you should respect their preferences. Cooking for others anytime, even at a backyard barbecue, is a serious responsibility. Your guests are there at your behest. Their happiness is in your hands!

Whether they be bosom friends or business acquaintances, your guests are, for the time being, your *confrères*, your *compadres*, your trusting companions — by definition, those people with whom you share bread (companion comes from the Latin *com-*, which means together, and *panis*, which means bread). Their only obligation, in the climate of ease and informality that you provide, is to accept your grill offerings and forget diner's decorum long enough to peel their shell-on shrimp without complaint and greedily lick their fingers afterwards.

The event is an exchange of great value: It's called friendship.

So before you put the steaks on to cook, be sure you and your guests are clearly of one mind regarding the terminology "rare," "medium" and "well-done." Is rare so raw as to be almost on the hoof? Are your friends in fact only looking for warmed through? Can you be sure that your medium is their rose pink? You can pray that they won't ask you to torch the meat, but if they do, and it pains you to do so — well, don't invite them back. Or better yet, serve them chicken, which is done when it's done and that's that.

NB: This is not a new battle. An old New England cookbook instructs that "rare done is the taste of this age." This was in the 1760s. And in *Duncan Hines' Food Odyssey*, which was published in 1955 (before Hines was a cake mix, he was a prominent restaurant reviewer in the U.S. who believed that "eating is more fun than anything else in the world"), the food writer singled out a steakhouse for favorable mention because its menu declared, "We are not responsible for any steak ordered well done."

Trail fare, reinvented: Succulent Barbecued Beef Ribs accompanied with zesty Cowpoke Baked Beans. Turn page for recipes.

PC 'Too Good To Be True!'
7 Bean Mix

Beans were a staple in the range diet, and they often made an appearance at both breakfast and dinner. Lazy cowpokes would throw a mess of beans uncleaned into a pot, let the chaff rise to the surface and the pebbles fall to the bottom, then cook them a good five hours over very low heat. That was the first round. The potful was enough to last three or four days, so each night our stalwart buckaroos would put the beans back on the fire — maybe tinker with them again — and ladle out some more. By the time they were scraping bottom, everyone would be crying about how they should have waited because the beans "was just gettin' good!"

Unlike those beans of yore, our Cowpoke Baked Beans are too good to last another day. They have a sweet-sour tang that'll set your tastebuds dancing, particularly when served with our irresistible Barbecued Beef Ribs.

In the unlikely event that you have any beans left over, they make a terrific lunch accompanied with thick slices of grilled PC Rustico Italian-Style White Bread.

BARBECUED BEEF RIBS

Beef ribs from a boned prime rib roast usually come three or four ribs per package at the supermarket. In some cases, it may be necessary to order ahead, particularly if you're feeding a crowd.

1	bottle (350 mL) PC Memories of Lyon 4-Peppercorn Sauce	1
1/2 cup	PC Memories of Kobe "The 2 Minute Miracle" Tamari Garlic Marinade	125 mL
2	onions, sliced	2
8 to 10 lb	meaty beef rib bones	4 to 5 kg

♦ Combine Memories of Lyon sauce, Memories of Kobe sauce and onions in large shallow dish. Add beef ribs and turn to coat well. Cover and let marinate in refrigerator for 2 to 4 hours. Let stand at room temperature for 30 minutes before cooking.

♦ Place ribs in shallow roasting pan and seal well with foil. Bake in 350°F (180°F) oven for 1 1/2 to 2 hours, or until meat starts to fall away from the bone.

♦ Remove ribs from pan, reserving cooking juices, and place on lightly greased grill over medium-high heat. Grill for 3 to 5 minutes per side, basting frequently with reserved juices. Cut into serving-size pieces. Serve with Cowpoke Baked Beans.

Makes 8 to 10 servings.

COWPOKE BAKED BEANS

Cowpokes — that's just another word for cowboys — called dried beans "prairie strawberries" because their varieties tended to be reddish brown kidney or pinto beans. If you have any cooked ribs from a previous night's barbecue, strip off the meat, dice and add to the beans before putting them into the oven.

PC 'Too Good To Be True!'
Great Northern Beans

8 oz	PC Naturally Smoked Bacon, chopped	250 g
2	medium onions, chopped	2
3	cloves PC Fresh Peeled Garlic, chopped	3
4	stalks celery, chopped	4
2	jars (each 28 oz/796 mL) PC 'Too Good To Be True!' Great Northern Beans, rinsed and drained	2
1	jar (28 oz/796 mL) PC 'Too Good To Be True!' 7 Bean Mix, rinsed and drained	1
1½ cups	PC La Elección del Presidente Extra-Chunky Salsa Picante, extra mild, mild, hot or volcano	375 mL
1 cup	PC Gourmet Barbecue Sauce	250 mL
½ cup	PC Dijon Mustard	125 mL
½ cup	molasses	125 mL
1	bottle (341 mL) PC Premium Draft Beer	1
¼ cup	chopped fresh parsley	50 mL
	Salt and freshly ground pepper	

• In large Dutch oven, cook bacon until tender, about 5 minutes. Add onions, garlic, celery and continue cooking until tender, about 10 minutes.
• Add great northern beans, 7 bean mix, salsa, barbecue sauce, Dijon mustard, molasses, beer, parsley and salt and pepper to taste. Transfer to 400°F (200°C) oven and cook for 2 hours, stirring frequently.
Makes 8 to 10 servings.

FOREMAN: *I'm a man of few words.*
If I say come, you come.
COWBOY: *I'm a man of few words, too.*
If I shake my head, I ain't comin'.

PC Esplendido
Flour Tortillas

Grill the steak, set out the tortillas, guacamole, chopped tomatoes, shredded lettuce, cheese and salsa, and your job is done. The great thing about fajitas (fa-HEE-tahs) — a meat and salad course all wrapped up in a soft warm tortilla — is that the guests get to assemble their own.

BEEF FAJITAS

The lime juice and balsamic vinegar impart a zesty flavor to the meat and tenderize it at the same time.

1/4 cup	PC Key West Lime Juice	50 mL
1/2 cup	PC Balsamic Vinegar	125 mL
2 tbsp	PC Naturally Brewed Soya Sauce	25 mL
1 tbsp	PC Chopped Garlic in Oil	15 mL
2 tbsp	PC Memories of Thailand Fiery Thai Dipping Sauce	25 mL
1/2 tsp	dried red pepper flakes	2 mL
1 tsp	salt	5 mL
1	flank steak (about 12 oz/375 g)	1
8	PC Esplendido Fajita Size Flour Tortillas	8
	Shredded lettuce	
	PC La Elección del Presidente Extra-Chunky Salsa Picante, hot or mild	
	PC La Elección del Presidente Frozen Guacamole, thawed Shredded Monterey Jack or Cheddar cheese	

• In medium-size bowl, combine lime juice, balsamic vinegar, soya sauce, garlic, Memories of Thailand sauce, red pepper flakes and salt. Add flank steak and turn to coat well. Cover and let marinate in refrigerator for 4 to 6 hours, preferably overnight.

• Place steak on grill over high heat and cook for 2 to 3 minutes per side or to desired doneness. Let rest about 5 minutes.

• Heat tortillas on the grill just until warmed through, about 15 seconds on each side.

• Thinly slice flank steak across the grain and serve with warmed tortillas, shredded lettuce, salsa, guacamole and shredded cheese.

Makes 4 servings.

PC Louisiana Hot Sauce

No matter what anyone tells you, salt meat before grilling. It ensures that the seasoning penetrates for better flavor. Yes, the salt will draw moisture to the surface of the meat (which is why some people abhor the practice), but it usually evaporates quickly over a hot fire.

▼

Some of the cookbook team flew to Memphis to sample the delights of the World Championship Barbecue Cooking Contest. A bunch of hobbyists called the Hogaholics — some of them lawyers, others self-professed hooligans, but all dissolute in their love of barbecue — prepared a fabulous Cajun-style ragoût of smoked mushrooms that they ladled over spaghetti. Here's our version, a choice addition to a perfectly grilled veal chop on a day when you're feeling extravagant.

GRILLED VEAL CHOPS WITH MUSHROOM RAGOÛT

We love the superb, smoky flavor of grilled mixed mushrooms in this outstanding dish, but it's also delicious with all white or cremini mushrooms. Use as an accompaniment to meat or spoon over pasta.

4	thick veal chops	4
	Salt and freshly ground pepper	
Mushroom Ragoût:		
8 oz	shiitake mushrooms	250 g
8 oz	portobello mushrooms	250 g
8 oz	oyster mushrooms	250 g
2	cloves PC Fresh Peeled Garlic	2
1 tbsp	PC Roasted Garlic-Flavored Olive Oil	15 mL
1	small onion, thinly sliced	1
1 cup	2% milk	250 mL
½ cup	whipping cream	125 mL
1 to 2 tsp	PC Louisiana Hot Sauce	5 to 10 mL
	Juice of ½ lemon	
	Salt and freshly ground pepper	

• Prepare Mushroom Ragoût first: Wipe mushrooms clean with damp cloth. Place in grill basket along with garlic. Cook over medium-high heat, turning periodically, until mushrooms are tender and lightly charred, about 15 minutes. Let cool and coarsely chop mushrooms and garlic. Set aside.
• In skillet over medium-high heat, heat roasted garlic oil. Add onion and cook a few minutes until tender. Reduce heat to medium low, stir in milk and cream and bring to boil; reduce heat and let simmer for 1 minute. Add mushrooms, roasted garlic, Louisiana hot sauce, lemon juice and salt and pepper to taste. Turn off heat.
• Season veal chops lightly with salt and pepper. On lightly greased grill over medium-high heat, grill chops for 5 to 7 minutes per side or to desired doneness. Arrange on individual plates.
• Heat mushroom mixture over medium heat for 1 to 2 minutes or just until heated through. Spoon over veal chops or serve on the side.
Makes 4 servings.

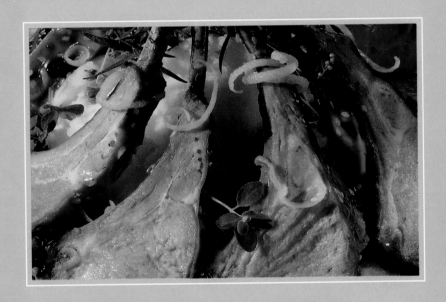

LAMB

Lightly crusted
outside, moist
and tender
inside: André's
Favorite Leg of
Lamb is perfumed
with garlic and
fresh rosemary.
Turn page for
this and other
lamb leg recipes.

PC Memories of Kyoto
Ginger Sauce

Leg of lamb, boned and butterflied, is André Gagné's preferred cut for a crowd. It's an unattractive lump when you see it laid out on the grill, but André, manager of Ziggys St. Clair Market in Toronto, says you'll be thankful for those varying thicknesses. He and his wife, Debra Mathews, a television producer, enjoy their lamb medium-rare, while some friends like the meat well-done. With lamb leg, "you get both in one piece."

André grew up an air force brat. Although both parents know their way around a kitchen, he says, "we always knew it was a special occasion when Dad was cooking. He'd talk about the incredible meals he'd enjoyed for about $10 when he was in Europe, like *coq au vin* (chicken in wine) and *boeuf bourguignon* (wine-braised beef), and then he'd try to recreate them at home."

Regular "bulk" cooking for four boys and a husband tended to be Mom's department. At age 12, André joined his Quebec-born father in the kitchen. Those experiences were early lessons in "good fresh ingredients, prepared simply," says André, a philosophy that carries over to the way he cooks today.

In his favorite lamb recipe, André marinates a boned and butterflied leg in buttermilk, an old *Insider's Report* trick, which he flavors with garlic and rosemary. "I usually leave it in the refrigerator for about 24 hours but once it went for 48 hours and the meat just melted in your mouth." As much as his parents love lamb, 4-year-old Christian isn't a fan yet. He prefers grilled sausage or an omelette.

ANDRÉ'S FAVORITE LEG OF LAMB

André Gagné, manager of Ziggys St. Clair Market, takes a classic Insider's Report *recipe one step further. Buttermilk acts as a meat tenderizer because it contains lactic acid.*

2 cups	buttermilk	500 mL
2 tbsp	chopped fresh rosemary	25 mL
2 tbsp	coarsely cracked pepper	25 mL
6	cloves PC Fresh Peeled Garlic, finely chopped	6
1	boned and butterflied leg of lamb (4 to 5 lb/2 to 2.5 kg)	1
¾ cup	PC Memories of Kyoto Ginger Sauce or PC Memories of Szechwan Peanut Sauce	175 mL

• In shallow glass dish, mix together buttermilk, rosemary, pepper and garlic.
• Add lamb and turn to coat all over. Cover and refrigerate 6 to 8 hours or, preferably, overnight. Turn lamb 3 or 4 times.
• On lightly greased grill over medium heat, cook lamb for about 15 to 18 minutes per side or until desired doneness, basting frequently with Memories of Kyoto or Memories of Szechwan sauce.
• Let lamb rest about 10 minutes, then slice across grain and serve on large platter.
Makes 6 servings.

A teriyaki marinade never fails to please. In the world of barbecue, it's the basic black suit — almost any meat or poultry wears it well. Our version, an adaptation of a favorite James Beard recipe, appeared in the first President's Choice cookbook.

Of all the meats, lamb seems to suffer the most loss of flavor and moisture when it is cooked to the well-done stage. (The meat will broadcast its demise by turning a dull, unappetizing greyish brown that's as dry in the mouth as it looks on the plate!) To enjoy rare meat *comme les français*, who have a great respect for lamb, stop the cooking when a meat thermometer inserted into the thickest part of the lamb registers 130°F (55°C). For medium doneness — the meat will be neither too rare or overly done but still tinged with pink and succulent — remove the lamb from the heat when its internal temperature reaches 140°F (60°C).

PC Memories of
Szechwan Peanut Sauce

MEMORIES OF JAMES BEARD
TERIYAKI LEG OF LAMB

You can use the same marinade for lamb steaks, beef tenderloin, pork ribs, blade steaks and cross-rib steaks. We prefer the PC Memories of Kobe sauce version for lamb and beef, and the soya sauce version for chicken and pork. The marinade can be reused if you bring it to a boil, then reduce the heat and let simmer for 5 minutes. Cool, then refrigerate, covered. Use within a week.

1 cup	PC Peanut Oil	250 mL
1 cup	PC Memories of Kobe "The 2 Minute Miracle" Tamari Garlic Marinade or PC Naturally Brewed Soya Sauce	250 mL
1 tbsp	PC Chopped Garlic in Oil	15 mL
1 tbsp	PC Puréed Ginger	15 mL
2/3 cup	dry sherry or Madeira wine	150 mL
1	boned and butterflied leg of lamb (4 to 5 lb/2 to 2.5 kg)	1

♦ Combine oil, Memories of Kobe sauce or soya sauce, garlic, ginger and sherry or Madeira.

♦ Place the lamb in a glass baking dish. Add Memories of Kobe mixture and turn lamb to coat all over. Cover and refrigerate 6 to 8 hours, preferably overnight; turn the lamb three or four times.

♦ Remove lamb from marinade and pat dry. On lightly greased grill over medium heat, cook lamb for about 15 to 18 minutes per side or until desired doneness, basting frequently with marinade.

♦ Let lamb rest about 10 minutes, then slice across grain into thin slices and serve on large platter.

Makes 6 servings.

CAROL'S LEG OF LAMB

BRUSH A BONED AND BUTTERFLIED LAMB LEG WITH PC EXTRA-VIRGIN OLIVE OIL. RUB WITH SALT AND PEPPER, CHOPPED FRESH GARLIC, CHOPPED FRESH ROSEMARY, PC BALSAMIC VINEGAR AND A LITTLE LEMON JUICE. MARINATE 1 TO 2 HOURS. PLACE ON GRILL OVER MEDIUM-HIGH HEAT AND COOK 15 TO 18 MINUTES PER SIDE OR TO DESIRED DONENESS. LET REST 10 MINUTES BEFORE SLICING. MAKES 6 SERVINGS.

PC Vague Memories of
Montego Bay The
Timid Jerk Marinade

Sometimes, a recipe looks too easy. If you like to putter around in the kitchen, you might be tempted to skip over it because there doesn't seem to be enough "happening" in the ingredient list. Our advice to you is: Do not let this lamb recipe slip by without trying it! It's simple, but it's unbelievably good.

You can use our PC Memories of Montego Bay Jerk Marinade, but frankly, this is one instance where PC Vague Memories of Montego Bay The Timid Jerk Marinade clearly won over our taste panelists. At the first tasting, half the lamb racks were marinated overnight in the mild sauce, half in the hot. Everybody agreed the milder version had a richer, more complex flavor.

JERK RACKS OF LAMB

Serve these spicy lamb racks with rice or couscous and grilled vegetables. The recommended beverage is our PC Premium Draft Beer.

| 1 | box (2³⁄₄ lb/1.2 kg) PC Frozen Frenched Racks of Spring Lamb (4 racks), thawed | 1 |
| 1 cup | (approx.) PC Vague Memories of Montego Bay The Timid Jerk Marinade | 250 mL |

• Cut lamb racks in half and trim off excess fat.
• Place in glass bowl. Add Vague Memories of Montego Bay marinade and toss to coat. Cover and let marinate in refrigerator for 6 to 8 hours or, preferably, overnight.
• Place lamb on lightly greased grill over medium-high heat and cook, turning and basting often with leftover jerk marinade, for 15 to 20 minutes or to desired doneness.
• Remove from grill and let rest 10 minutes before serving.
Makes 4 servings.

PC Memories of
Hong Kong Spicy Black
Bean and Garlic Sauce

▲

TOASTED
SESAME SEEDS
—————
PLACE SEEDS ON
SMALL BAKING SHEET
AND TOAST IN
350°F (180°C) OVEN
FOR 3 TO 5 MINUTES
OR UNTIL GOLDEN
BROWN, SHAKING PAN
ONCE OR TWICE.
WATCH CAREFULLY TO
AVOID BURNING.

▼

Our President's Choice development chefs worked closely with the hotel kitchen at Toronto's Sutton Place, now a Meridien hotel, to develop the dishes served in its Sanssouci restaurant and Alexandra's pasta bar as a special tribute to the *Insider's Report* on its 10th anniversary.

Among the most popular of these "President's Choice" dishes was a main dish created especially for the occasion, Grilled Racks of Lamb with Ginger & Black Bean Sauce, made with three distinctly different "Memories of . . ." sauces: Kyoto Ginger, Hong Kong Spicy Black Bean and Garlic, and Jaipur Curry & Passion Fruit.

This is a spectacular way to present rack of lamb, and even though the trinity of sauces sounds risqué, if not downright threatening to the tastebuds, the flavors come together beautifully.

GRILLED LAMB RACKS WITH GINGER & BLACK BEAN SAUCE

Don't skip the toasted sesame seeds. They add to the drama of this dish and provide an appealing crunch.

1 cup	PC Memories of Kyoto Ginger Sauce	250 mL
1/4 cup	PC Memories of Hong Kong Spicy Black Bean and Garlic Sauce	50 mL
1/4 cup	PC Memories of Jaipur Curry & Passion Fruit Sauce	50 mL
1/4 cup	dry sherry	50 mL
1 tbsp	grated orange peel	15 mL
1/4 cup	toasted sesame seeds (see sidebar)	50 mL
1	box (2³/₄ lb/1.2 kg) PC Frozen Frenched Racks of Spring Lamb (4 racks), thawed	1

• In mixing bowl, combine Memories of Kyoto, Hong Kong and Jaipur sauces. Add sherry, orange peel and sesame seeds.
• Place lamb in sauce mixture and turn to coat well. Cover and let marinate in refrigerator for 6 to 8 hours or overnight.
• On lightly greased grill over medium-high heat, cook lamb racks, turning and brushing with marinade, for 12 to 15 minutes or to desired doneness.
• Place remaining marinade in saucepan and heat until boiling. Serve as sauce with lamb.
Makes 4 servings.

PC Memories of Jaipur
Curry &
Passion Fruit Sauce

I ndian cooking is intoxicating in its spicing and rarely fails to evoke the drama of the spice trade that opened ocean routes to the East. It cannot be reduced to curry powders in jars, many of which are top-heavy with the distinctive, one-dimensional flavor of turmeric, an underground rhizome or stem that's related to ginger. Real curry — from *kari*, which means sauce — is a blending of many sweet and aromatic spices, of which the bitter, slightly mustardy flavor of turmeric is only one note among the balance of many. Formulas vary according to the personal tastes and culinary heritage of the cook.

The inspiration for our President's Choice Memories of Jaipur Curry & Passion Fruit Sauce came from the kitchens of the Rambagh Palace Hotel in Jaipur — a curry sauce not easily duplicated, but we think we've come close! In our opinion, it's heaven in a bottle. If your only experience with curry has been the powder you spoon from a jar, then you owe it to yourself to try this sauce. Curried Lamb Chops make a fine introduction, as does our Curried Chicken Sandwich (see p. 202).

CURRIED LAMB CHOPS

Yogurt mint sauce is a refreshing counterpoint to the heat of the curry sauce and it cools down the mouth. In India, a yogurt-based salad called raita *often accompanies highly seasoned dishes. The cool hint of mint permeating these chops comes from the President's Choice Mint Sauce in the marinade.*

1	box (2½ lb/1.1 kg) PC Frozen Frenched-Style Shoulder Racks of Lamb (4 racks), thawed	1
1 cup	PC Memories of Jaipur Curry & Passion Fruit Sauce	250 mL
1 cup	PC All-Natural Light (1% M.F.) Plain Yogurt	250 mL
¼ cup	PC Mint Sauce	50 mL
1 tbsp	PC Chopped Garlic in Oil	15 mL

• With sharp knife, slice each lamb rack between bones to produce 16 chops in total.
• Mix together Memories of Jaipur sauce, yogurt, mint sauce and garlic. Place half the mixture in a small container and refrigerate for later use as sauce to accompany these chops. Place remaining mixture in shallow pan; add lamb chops and toss to coat well. Cover and let marinate in refrigerator for at least 4 to 6 hours, preferably overnight.
• On lightly greased grill over medium-high heat, cook chops for 5 to 6 minutes per side or to desired doneness, basting often with leftover marinade. Serve with reserved sauce mixture.
Makes 4 to 6 servings.

PC 'Too Good To Be True!' Tzatziki Low-Fat Yogurt Dip & Spread

It is not really an exaggeration to say that peace and happiness begin, geographically, where garlic is used in cooking.

— Marcel Boulestin

The Ottoman Turks had 400 years to influence the course of cuisine in Greece, which they occupied from 1450 to 1821. Consequently, many traditional Greek foods bear a Turkish imprint — for example, shish kebabs (skewered meat) and yogurt (which means "to thicken" in Turkish). The Turks used their own language to describe traditional foods such as the Greek garlicky yogurt dip made with garlic and cucumbers. They called this pungent mixture *tzatziki* (tsad-TSEE-kee).

Our 'Too Good To Be True!' Tzatziki Low-Fat Yogurt Dip & Spread has the traditional flavor of the Greek dip but doesn't have as high a milk fat content because it's made with pressed non-fat yogurt. So while it's thick, its butterfat content is only 2% — significantly less than the 15% milk fat that you'll find in a similar commercial product here at home.

'TOO EASY TO BE TRUE!' LAMB KEBABS

With only 11 calories per tablespoon (15 mL), PC tzatziki is perfect on roasted potatoes or as a dip for vegetables and crusty bread. It's also a flavorful marinade for lamb kebabs. Serve this excellent dish with grilled vegetables and couscous salad.

1	tub (250 g) PC 'Too Good To Be True!' Tzatziki Low-Fat Yogurt Dip & Spread	1
2 tbsp	chopped fresh rosemary	25 mL
	Salt and freshly ground pepper	
2 lb	lean lamb, cut in 2-inch (5 cm) cubes	1 kg

♦ Mix together tzatziki, rosemary and salt and pepper to taste. Add lamb cubes and toss to coat. Cover and marinate in refrigerator for 6 to 8 hours or overnight.

♦ Thread lamb onto skewers. Place on lightly greased grill over medium-high heat and cook for 3 to 5 minutes per side or to desired doneness.

Makes 4 to 6 servings.

L amb ribs are common barbecue fare in South Africa, but they're virtually unknown on this side of the Atlantic. They're also popular among Pacific islanders, who cook them according to traditional methods: Wrapped in leaves or buried amidst hot stones in the ground. PC frozen lamb ribs are cut exclusively for us from New Zealand spring lamb and are as easy to cook as pork ribs. As with pork ribs, steaming lamb ribs before you put them on the grill makes them tender to the bite.

SZECHWAN LAMB RIBS

For a variation, glaze lamb ribs with PC Tournament Barbecue Sauce. It's a perfect complement.

1	pkg (3.2 lb/1.4 kg) PC Frozen New Zealand Spring Lamb Ribs (8 racks), thawed	1
1	bottle (455 mL) PC Szechwan Peanut Barbecue Sauce	1

• In large pot, arrange ribs on steamer rack over (not in) boiling water. Return water to boil, cover pan and steam ribs over medium-high heat for about 1 hour or until meat starts to fall off the bone. (Be careful not to let pan dry out; add more boiling water as necessary.)
• On greased grill over medium-hot coals, arrange ribs meat-side down and cook 1 to 2 minutes or until some of the fat has burned off. Brush ribs all over with barbecue sauce and cook, turning and basting often, for about 8 to 10 minutes or until ribs start to char and caramelize.
• Brush again just before removing from grill.
Makes 4 servings.

*Tin plates last longer
'cause they're easy to straighten out
after a boisterous meal.*

—old cowboy saying

PC Frozen
New Zealand Spring
Lamb Ribs

▲

RAY "RED" GILL,
CHIEF COOK FOR THE
ARKANSAS RAZORBACK
COOKERS (HIS VARIED
CAREER INCLUDES STINTS
AS RODEO COWBOY,
STEER WRESTLER AND
CALF ROPER), WON TOP
HONORS AT THE 1993
TORONTO RIBFEST
BY BASTING BEEF RIBS
WITH 1 CUP (250 mL)
PC TOURNAMENT
BARBECUE SAUCE AND
1/2 CUP (125 mL)
PC LA ELECCIÓN DEL
PRESIDENTE EXTRA
CHUNKY SALSA PICANTE.

▼

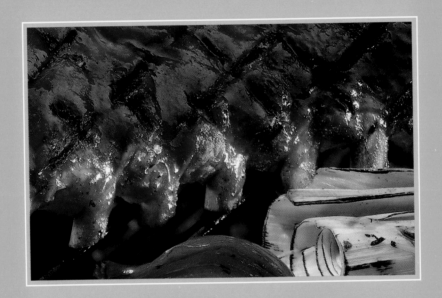

PORK

MEMPHIS MEMOIRS

Anyone familiar with the rites and rituals of barbecue knows that almost equal in importance to the actual taste of the 'cue is the amount and quality of the mumbo jumbo you put out while barbecuing.

— C. Schlesinger and J. Willoughby, *The Thrill of the Grill,* ©1990

MEMPHIS, Tenn. — There are more than 60 places to eat barbecue in Memphis. But the one that matters most in this self-proclaimed barbecue capital of the world — a city named after the ancient Egyptian capital on the Nile but remembered more for its musical heroes — is in the centre of town, where for three days each spring, fun-lovers, fame-seekers and professional barbecue cooks go hog wild on the east bank of the Mississippi. This is the World Championship Barbecue Contest, the signature event in the monthlong international celebration called Memphis in May.

Teams who sign up for the barbecue competition set up their booths in Tom Lee Park, literally right where the river flows past the city's front doorstep; right where the birthplace of blues, historic Beale Street, stops at the banks. There's a slim spit of sand in the middle of this mighty river, and it's overgrown with weeping willows. One day in 1925, Tom Lee, a field hand and levee worker, had been out pruning willows such as these. Tom was on his way home in a small company motorboat when he came upon a sinking excursion steamer about 16 miles (25 km) downstream from Memphis. A group of engineers and their families had been out touring the levee system, which had successfully withstood the spring floodwaters.

"Sensibilist drowning folks I ever saw," Tom later told the local newspaper. "They didn't lose their heads, jes' waited for me to come get 'em." He ferried 32 people across, two and three at a time, but 23 others perished in the swift muddy waters. The engineers' club was so grateful for Tom's rescue effort — the humble laborer couldn't even swim — that they bought him and his wife a house. He died in 1952 at the age of 67. Two years later, a park in the heart of Memphis was renamed in his honor.

As we survey the park, there's nothing pastoral here, nothing green down by the riverside. It's plain dirt underfoot and the strong gusts coming across the water are blowing up dust.

Many of this year's participants cook out of converted oil drums, while others with more daring and showmanship shovel their pork ribs and shoulders into custom cookers masquerading as teapots or locomotives or airplanes. Those of refinement construct elaborate two-storey frame structures with roof gardens that allow for lazy lingering, or don black ties and tails and dress their tables with white linen. If their food doesn't cut it with the judges, they might at least walk away with first prize for Best Area, although that honor carries less prize money ($200) than either Showmanship ($500) or Hog Calling ($300). At a pigfest of this magnitude, you have to keep your priorities straight.

There are approximately 30 other annual North American barbecue contests sanctioned by the Memphis group and governed by its rules. Barbecuers with wanderlust can wing it to Lisdoonvarna, Ireland, for the Irish Cup Invitational Barbecue Festival, or the network of contests held in New Zealand and Thailand, all of which draw regulars from the Memphis circuit.

But Memphis is the Big One. Memphis is the Ultimate Good Time.

We're here for the 17th annual event, which has attracted more than 250 teams. A more boisterous bunch of barbecuers you won't find! Teams with names like Rowdy Southern Swine, Arkansas Outbackers, Ribberboat Gamblers, Backwood Boys, Ribticklers, Virginia Swine & Dine, Fat Boys from Beale, the Middle Aged Mutant Ninja Porkers, Choo Chew Bar-B-Que, the Pit & the Pigulum II, and Oink, Cackle & Moo. Most of them come from the traditional barbecue states of the American south — Texas, Missouri, North Carolina, Kansas, Georgia, Arkansas and Tennessee. Especially Tennessee. Tennesseans outnumber the others by almost two to one.

Ireland is here this year. So is Canada for about the eighth year running (alas, no wins yet), represented by the Collingwood Boarmasters. There's even a team from the Ivory Coast, this year's honored guests. In previous years, Estonia, Norway, Australia and New Zealand have sent teams. Everyone comes to have fun; cooking is something they do on the side.

There are three main categories for judging: Shoulder, Rib and Whole Hog. A fourth, Patio Porkers, is where they place novice teams or plain folk who just want to grab their cookers and get cookin'. The competing teams are fairly cloistered; their grub is not for consumption by the masses. This is a competition, remember. A dozen judges pick their way through food prepared by the competing teams while five winners from previous years cook for the public: Ribs by the pair or the slab, plus shoulder by the ounce, pound or in a sandwich.

And in case that's not enough, elsewhere in the park, which stretches for about eight city blocks, licensed concessionaires dispense sausages, gyros, souvlaki, barbecued bologna sandwiches, hot dogs, pizza, chips, funnel cakes (sort of like deep-fried dough strips), snow cones, Italian ices, cotton candy, cola and coffee. In a small stand erected by Louis Martin III, chef-owner of the Turkey Express in Memphis, barbecued turkey drumsticks the size of forearms lay heaped in piles, glistening dusky mahogany beneath the red glow of the warming lamps. Louis's special turkey seasoning contains 14 spices. He was a supermarket meat cutter before going into business for himself.

Make no mistake, Memphis in May is a serious pig-out. One comes prepared for hand-to-mouth contact with the biggest single concentration of barbecued foods in the world.

Mid-morning, we watch transfixed as one of the competitors cracks a few eggs into a huge cast-iron pan at least as wide as his arm is long and leaves them to fry sunny-side up in a pitch black cooker that he fashioned out of a 55-gallon oil drum. The lemon yellow yolks are brilliant against the inky blackness of the pan. Mark is from Milan, Tennessee, which is halfway between Memphis and Nashville. Pronounce that MY-lan. "This is south of the Mason-Dixon line so we got to drawl it out," he says. "That way you can distinguish it's a lo-o-o-ng way from Italy." The whites of the eggs start to curl at the edges. Grease-stained ruffles encircling sunny orbs. Mark offers us some "Tennessee breakfast," which turns out not to be eggs at all, but an amber liquid with close flavor ties to moonshine. He and his teammates will get the eggs.

One of the paradoxes of slow cooking barbecue, given the noose of contest rules governing it today, is its spontaneity. People in the mid-South say that pork barbecue used to be cooked on an old bedspring. They would set it over a fire, throw on a hog and then cover the whole lot with an old car hood to hold in the vital smoke. Worked just fine.

Even today, pros with custom cookers will fall back on the tried-and-true alternative upon which many of them first learned their art: An iron grate secured by concrete cinder blocks with a piece of sheet metal to act as a cover. Jim Ward, chief cook for the Federal Express Porky Pilots, did just that in 1993 and came first in Whole Hog. This is his team's 12th time out. (They've twice taken first place for Whole Hog.) This year, the hog is back on the team's custom cooker and the air is thick with the smell and smoke from hickory sawdust. Bagfuls of it are fed into the cooker's wood compartment by one of his teammates and then rolled back under the fire. It's a gritty eye-searing job but someone's got to do it.

Over at No. 130 in the rib camp, we discover the world's tallest barbecue chef, "Big Joe," standing a modest seven feet even in front of his custom cooker, the Joe Drilling Barbecue Team Grill. Essentially it's a modified kettle smoker that combines smoke and steam. There's a firebox on the bottom, water pipes to humidify the smoke, and a grid on top to hold the food. It took 1½ years to construct and it holds 300 pounds (136 kg) of meat. Good thing. Big Joe and his 13 teammates from Little Rock, Arkansas, expect to feed 300 this night alone.

Big Joe explains how his grill works. It sounds like mumbo jumbo to us. "The twin turbo chargers force feed a 30% O.D. 14:71 blower a healthy diet of 97% nitromethane and 3% alcohol," he says. "Digestion is handled by 48 valves and 12 perfectly matched 14:5:1 pistons. Exhaust is via two 5-inch dump tubes." All of this, he assures us, combines to deliver a staggering 7,200 horsepower at 9,000 RPM. Later, Big Joe takes it all back. What he said about the grill wasn't exactly true. Say what?! Outlandish talk is one of the rites of barbecue, we learn, like haggling in the marketplace. But he's fierce on this point: "It does cook the finest meat you'll ever eat at anytime, anywhere!"

We stop at No. 177, Apple City BB-Q, the premier rib cookers from Murphysboro, Illinois, and two-time Grand Champion winners (in 1990, their first time out, and 1992). Chief cook Mike Mills says they won't be back. "This is our last competition," he tells us. But then, they've won just about every contest they've entered over a five-year period.

Mike has a restaurant in southern Illinois that's practically in an apple orchard, figuratively speaking, so they use grated apples and apple juice in the sauce and green applewood prunings to flavor the fire. Since smoke is the soul of their barbecue, they skin their pork back ribs of the tough membrane that would otherwise prevent smoke from penetrating — they do this with each of the 40-odd slabs they prepare at a time.

Mike's theory, which was passed down from his Dad, is that pork smokes best at temperatures just low enough to keep the meat's surface from cooking. (Once the surface is cooked, it acts as a protective barrier and doesn't allow as much of the smoke to penetrate the heart of the meat, he contends.)

After smoking for about two hours at a "cool" 140°F (60°C), the temperature is hiked and the ribs are left to "sweat," which concentrates the smoke even further. The ribs are then rubbed with Apple City's secret blend of 18 different ingredients, the one Mike calls Magic Dust, then held at 200°F (95°C) for about 6½ hours or until done. During the last 30 minutes, they're mopped with a vinegar-based sauce, which immediately classifies them as wet-dry ribs.

We don't get to taste the result, since there won't be any ready until closer to judging time. (It's not just time that's invested in Memphis; it's a big expense buying the food to cook. Most teams are sponsored, usually by an employer or a food or beverage company or some other member of the hospitality industry. Even the U.S. Postal Service has kicked in.) It's a shame to leave No. 177, however, since Apple City BB-Q's surroundings are so inviting. All white trim and red apple icons. And spacious by the standards governing pavilions here. One could pull up a chair and daydream in the cool shade, happy for a respite from the afternoon sun. The next coolest place to be is in the river itself.

But move on we do, as we've heard the Irish are here. The Leprechaun Cookers are No. 372 on the competition site. (The Irish were the largest group of immigrants to Memphis in the 1840s.) Johnny, John G. and Sean have fish, fowl, spring lamb and pork butt on their menu, but the team from Shannon, Ireland, is primarily here to show off their shoulders. The fish *does* sound tantalizing. "Irish sea halibut," we're told when we ask what kind. And how do you plan to cook it? "In foil, with white wine." When can we taste some? "Come back tonight." For sure. We return that evening but the advice was bad, or maybe it was Irish blarney. There'll be no fish until tomorrow.

The lesson here in Memphis is that there's no single best way to barbecue. However, if you categorized the barbecuers on site, you could force them all under one umbrella: Smokers. Smoke is the soul of barbecue. Splitting hairs yields finer distinctions; participants decide to be either "dry" (they use spices) or "wet" (they like their sauce) or both. Over at The Trading Post, the Pit Bosses are generously applying a dry rub to both sides of their ribs. Sauce comes later. They're doing pork loins, too, but they've had to speed up the process: The loins are foil-wrapped and cooked at 250°F (120°C) for 2 hours; then smoked for 1½ hours. It's the only way they'll be able to cook enough to feed the crowds later.

More than 75,000 people tramped through the 17th annual barbecue fest in Memphis. Once again, Apple City BB-Q won Grand Champion and came in first for Ribs.

Porky Pilots placed third in Whole Hog but that's OK. There were other rewards; by the time the results were tabulated, NBC's Willard Scott had already interviewed the team for the *Today* show.

Big Joe's team didn't win a thing even though Joe figures they cooked up their best ribs ever. It's the way things happen. Veterans know it's not just the food. It also matters who shakes whose hand, who's judging and whether the judges like what they hear when the teams expound on their barbecue theory. A tenth of a point can make all the difference in where you place. But the devil gets his due. After Memphis, Joe headed to the Festival for the Pig in Oklahoma. His team took first for Ribs, first for Shoulder and Grand Champion overall.

It matters not how simple the food . . . but let it be of
good quality and properly cooked,
and everyone who partakes of it will enjoy it.

—Alexis Soyer
The Modern Housewife, 1851

PC Dijon Mustard

If you grill today's pork until it's grey through and through, you'll be eating shoe leather. Pork is 23% leaner on average than it was even 15 years ago, so it needs gentler handling. New breeding methods have made pork safe to eat when its internal temperature reaches 150°F (65°C). At this temperature, there may still be a faint pink cast to the meat, so don't be alarmed.

GRILLED PORK CHOPS WITH BASIL

Canadian pork is recognized for its quality and is exported all over the world, particularly to Japan.

3 tbsp	PC Extra-Virgin Olive Oil	45 mL
1/2 cup	dry white wine	125 mL
2 tbsp	fresh lemon juice	25 mL
1 tbsp	PC Dijon Mustard	15 mL
2 tbsp	finely chopped shallots	25 mL
2 tbsp	chopped fresh basil	25 mL
	Freshly ground pepper	
4	pork loin chops, about 3/4 inch (2 cm) thick	4

• In shallow glass dish, mix together olive oil, wine, lemon juice, mustard, shallots, basil and pepper to taste. Add pork chops and turn to coat. Cover and let marinate in refrigerator for 4 to 6 hours, turning once or twice.
• Place chops on lightly greased grill over medium heat and cook for 5 to 7 minutes per side or until outside is golden brown and inside has a faint hint of pink. Serve with Grilled Honey Onions.
Makes 4 servings.

GRILLED HONEY ONIONS

You can substitute Vidalia onions in this superb dish. And if you like, you can cut onions crosswise into 1/4-inch (5 mm) slices.

2	red onions	2
1/2 cup	PC Premium Alfalfa Honey	125 mL
2 tbsp	PC Naturally Brewed Soya Sauce	25 mL
2 tbsp	PC Dijon Mustard	25 mL

• Slice tops off onions and peel, making sure to keep root end intact.
• Slice onions in half vertically through root. Cut each half into 4 to 6 wedges, cutting through root so wedges hold together.
• In medium-size bowl, mix together honey, soya sauce and Dijon mustard. Add onion pieces and toss to coat. Let marinate for 1 to 2 hours.
• Place onion wedges in grill basket and grill over medium-high heat, turning occasionally, for 10 to 15 minutes or until tender and lightly charred.
Makes 4 servings.

PC Ranch Dressing

A HEAVY-DUTY PLASTIC
BAG IS IDEAL FOR
MARINATING. TIE IT
OFF CLOSE TO THE FOOD
AND TURN THE BAG
FROM TIME TO TIME
TO ENSURE THAT THE
MEAT OR POULTRY
MARINATES EVENLY. THE
LONGER THE MARINATING
TIME, THE MORE
INTENSE THE FLAVOR.

▼

P ork loin has a close, dense texture that requires extra care to keep it moist. Perfectly cooked, it can be as succulent as expensive veal. Overcooked, it will be dry and tough and have an unappetizing grey cast.

Knowing that some people won't even venture to cook pork loin because of the consequences of overcooking, we developed this simple recipe designed to keep the meat moist and show it off for all its riches. The secret is the combination of PC Ranch Dressing and PC Memories of Kobe "The 2 Minute Miracle" Tamari Garlic Marinade, which enhances the flavor of pork as successfully as it works miracles on beef.

KOBE RANCH PORK LOIN

The roast will continue to cook after it's removed from the grill, so be sure to remove it at the specified internal temperature or a few minutes before.

1	PC Frozen Danish Pork Loin (4 to 5 lb/2 to 2.5 kg), thawed	1
2 tbsp	PC Tellicherry Black Peppercorns	25 mL
2 cups	PC Ranch Dressing	500 mL
3/4 cup	PC Memories of Kobe "The 2 Minute Miracle" Tamari Garlic Marinade	175 mL

• Using sharp knife, score top of pork loin in diamond pattern.

• Wrap peppercorns in a tea towel and, using a heavy skillet or hammer, give a couple of good thwacks to coarsely crack the pepper. Sprinkle pork all over with cracked pepper and, using the heel of your hand, press pepper into meat.

• Place pork loin in heavy plastic bag; add ranch dressing and Memories of Kobe marinade. Seal well, turn a few times to coat meat with marinade and let marinate in refrigerator for 6 to 8 hours or overnight, turning occasionally.

• Place pork loin on lightly greased grill over high heat and cook for 2 to 3 minutes per side or until meat is seared all over. Reduce heat to medium and cook with lid down for 40 to 50 minutes, or until internal temperature reaches 150°F (65°C) on meat thermometer; turn and baste meat 2 or 3 times during cooking. Meat will have just a hint of pink in the centre when it's done. Let stand for 10 to 15 minutes before slicing.
Makes 8 to 10 servings.

PC Memories of Hawaii
Polynesian Sweet &
Sour Sauce

The longest shish kebab in the world measured 1,000 feet 8 inches (305 m) and was assembled by a newspaper team in Pietermaritzburg, South Africa. You won't beat their record for length with these kebabs, but you're sure to set a new standard for taste.

Souvlaki (soo-VLAH-kee) is what the Greeks call shish kebab — *souvlá* means spit or skewer — and theirs, herb-perfumed and grilled over an aromatic charcoal fire, is the finest to be had anywhere in the world. Our kitchen came up with this excellent variation using sage. The PC Memories of Hawaii Polynesian Sweet & Sour Sauce is an unusual touch. Be warned, there is no substitute!

SOUVLAKI WITH ROASTED GARLIC OIL

Fresh sage gives these skewers of pork a clean fresh flavor. The fresh herb is more delicate in flavor than the dried product, so feel comfortable using the maximum amount called for in this recipe.

3/4 cup	PC Memories of Hawaii Polynesian Sweet & Sour Sauce	175 mL
1/4 cup	PC Roasted Garlic-Flavored Olive Oil	50 mL
1 tbsp	PC Chopped Garlic in Oil	15 mL
2 tbsp	chopped shallot	25 mL
1/4 cup	finely chopped green onions	50 mL
1 to 2 tbsp	chopped fresh sage	15 to 30 mL
1 to 2 tbsp	chopped fresh thyme	15 to 30 mL
1 tbsp	freshly ground pepper	15 mL
2 lb	pork loin, cut in 1 1/2-inch (4 cm) cubes	1 kg
8 to 12	pita breads	8 to 12
	PC 'Too Good To Be True!' Tzatziki Low-Fat Yogurt Dip & Spread	

◆ In mixing bowl, combine Memories of Hawaii sauce, garlic-flavored oil, chopped garlic, shallot, green onions, sage, thyme and pepper. Add pork cubes and toss to coat well. Cover and let marinate in refrigerator for 6 to 8 hours or overnight.

◆ Soak wooden skewers in water for about 30 minutes. Thread pork cubes onto skewers.

◆ Place skewers on lightly greased grill over medium-high heat and cook, turning occasionally, for 12 to 15 minutes, or until pork has only the slightest hint of pink in the centre. A few minutes before pork is finished cooking, place pita breads on the grill and warm for about 1 minute, turning once.

◆ Serve pork cubes with warm pita breads and tzatziki.

Makes 4 to 6 servings.

PC Tournament
Barbecue Sauce

▲

BACK RIBS, WHICH

COME FROM THE BACK OF

THE HOG, ARE SMALLER

BUT MEATIER THAN

SPARERIBS, WHICH COME

FROM THE BELLY.

THEY'RE ALSO NOT AS

FATTY AS SPARERIBS AND

THEIR MEAT IS MORE

TENDER. SOME PEOPLE

PREFER SPARERIBS,

CLAIMING THEIR EXTRA

FAT GIVES THEM

THE PROPER SUCCULENCE.

(FAT IN MEAT IS A GREAT

CARRIER OF FLAVOR.)

▼

Ribs are done when "you can take 'em and break 'em," as the experts say. That's their measure of tender, succulent eating — and it's easy enough to achieve when you prepare ribs according to this recipe. The directions come from product developer and chef Ted Reader, who loves schmoozing with the pros when he heads south to the ribfests, those annual barbecue competitions that bring together hundreds of professional rib cookers vying for cash prizes.

On one of his trips, Ted met Jerry Gibson of Ohio, who divulged his backyard barbecue secret for making super ribs using some of the tricks he learned on the circuit: Start with back ribs, give them a "dry rub" for extra flavor and then precook them in the oven to shorten grill time and render out much of the fat, which causes flare-ups.

Match them with our PC Tournament Barbecue Sauce and your ribs will taste so good they'll "make you wanna howl at the moon."

BARBECUED BACK RIBS

These are table-thumping good. The secret is our PC Tournament Barbecue Sauce, a gourmet sweet-and-sour blend that won the trophy for Best Sauce at Ottawa's 1993 Ribfest. It beat out the competition from Alabama (where they know plenty about barbecue!) and as far away as Australia.

4	racks pork back ribs (each about 1½ lb/750 g)	4
4 tbsp	PC Spicy Barbecue Seasoning	60 mL
12	thin slices fresh lemon	12
1	bottle (455 mL) PC Tournament Barbecue Sauce	1

♦ Rub ribs all over with spicy barbecue seasoning.
♦ Arrange ribs meat-side down in large roasting pan, overlapping as necessary to fit pan. Place lemon slices on top. (The acid in lemon helps tenderize meat.)
♦ Pour in water to a depth of ½ inch (1 cm). Cover pan with foil and place in 325°F (160°C) oven for about 2½ hours or until meat pulls away cleanly from the bone.
♦ Place on well-greased grill over medium-high heat for a few minutes until ribs are crispy and deep brown in color.
♦ Continue cooking, turning and brushing often with barbecue sauce, for 10 to 15 minutes until ribs are slightly charred, but not burned.
♦ Remove from grill and brush lightly with more sauce. Slice between ribs and serve.
Makes 4 to 6 servings.

Dressed-up dogs, from left: Coney Island Chili Dog, Tex-Mex Dog with Guacamole & Salsa, Oktoberfest Ham Dog with cheesy sauerkraut topping. Turn page for recipes.

PC Cheddar Smokie
Wieners

Do you know anyone who is able to consume multiple Super Colossal Kobe Burger Stacks (see p. 66) without ever coming up for air? Then you're probably dealing with a graduate of the President's Choice Eating Dynamics Institute.

"PC Marathon Eaters," as we call them, are easy to spot. They can eat many of their favorite PC foods in one sitting — or, more likely, standing. They can eat in any direction — up or down, right to left, it doesn't matter. Barely finished with one course, they're usually sniffing out the next. Worthy of their name, they can eat four times as much as anyone else in half the time! Marathon Eaters have all the necessary skills for stockpiling their favorite foods (you may recognize the hollow legs or bottomless pits).

You never know when one of these eaters-in-training might come your way. But by their eating habits, you shall know them. A Marathon Eater may already be in your midst, perhaps a member of your own family?! So be prepared, especially for your barbecues. Fresh air makes appetites grow.

TEX-MEX DOGS WITH GUACAMOLE & SALSA

Real Cheddar cheese makes our PC Cheddar Smokie Wieners a hit with hot dog fans.

8	PC Cheddar Smokie Wieners	8
8	PC Esplendido Fajita Size Flour Tortillas	8
2 cups	shredded lettuce	500 mL
1 cup	alfalfa sprouts	250 mL
1/2 cup	PC La Elección del Presidente Frozen Guacamole, thawed	125 mL
1/2 cup	PC La Elección del Presidente Extra-Chunky Salsa Picante, hot or mild	125 mL

• Place wieners on lightly greased grill over medium-high heat for a few minutes, turning occasionally, until heated through and lightly charred.
• Shortly before wieners are done, add tortillas to grill and heat for 20 to 30 seconds per side.
• Lay tortillas flat on work surface. Top each with lettuce and alfalfa sprouts. Place a wiener in the centre of each. Spoon on guacamole and salsa.
• Fold sides of tortilla over filling, overlapping more at bottom to form cone shape and hold filling in place.
Makes 4 to 8 servings.

Oktoberfest Ham Dogs

The hot dog is a German-Americanism, a Frankfurt-style sausage in a bun. A German immigrant introduced the concept in St. Louis in the 1880s, but it didn't catch on until after the World's Fair in 1904, when a cartoonist drew a sausage shaped like a Dachshund and the "hot dog" was born.

2 cups	PC Hofbräu Sauerkraut, drained	500 mL
1 cup	grated Swiss Emmenthal cheese	250 mL
¼ cup	PC Dijon Mustard Mayo Sauce	50 mL
	or PC Dijon Mustard	
8	PC Ham Dogs Ham Wieners	8
8	hot dog buns, plain or with caraway	8

◆ In small saucepan, mix together sauerkraut, grated cheese and Dijon mayo sauce. Heat, stirring, over low heat until hot. Turn off heat.
◆ Heat ham dogs on lightly greased grill over medium heat for a few minutes, turning occasionally, until hot and lightly charred. Just before wieners are done heating, place buns on grill for about 1 minute until lightly toasted.
◆ Place ham dogs on buns. Spoon sauerkraut mixture on top.
Makes 4 to 8 servings.

Coney Island Chili Dogs

Our PC cheese-in-a-can is made with real, extra sharp Canadian Cheddar cheese. It's great on hot dogs and burgers – you can also squeeze it on tacos and crackers.

1	pkg (65 g) PC 'Too Good To Be True!' Instant Vegetarian Chili	1
	Boiling water	
8	PC Hot Dog Wieners	8
8	top-sliced hot dog buns, lightly buttered	8
	PC "Ready, Aim, Cheese!" Pasteurized Process Cheese Spread	

◆ Prepare vegetarian chili: Pull back lid halfway across top of cup. Fill cup with boiling water, stir well and return lid to original position. Let stand for 5 to 7 minutes, stirring occasionally.
◆ Place wieners on lightly greased grill over medium heat for a few minutes, turning occasionally, until heated through and lightly charred.
◆ Just before wieners are done, add buns to grill and heat for a minute until lightly toasted.
◆ Place wieners in buns. Spoon chili over each. Spray on "Ready, Aim, Cheese!" and serve.
Makes 4 to 8 servings.

PC Ham Dogs Ham Wieners

▲

HOT DOGS HAVE BEEN AROUND NORTH AMERICA SINCE THE 1880s, BUT IT WAS 20 YEARS LATER THAT CONEY ISLAND HOT DOG VENDORS INCORPORATED THEM INTO THE CULINARY LANDSCAPE. WHEN HOT DOGS GOT A CHILI TOPPING, OR "CONEY SAUCE," THEY BECAME KNOWN AS CHILI DOGS. CHEESE IS AN ESSENTIAL COMPONENT.

▼

POULTRY

PC 100% Pure
Maple Syrup

Throughout the centuries, the foods earmarked for feasts and celebrations of various magnitudes, from birthdays to weddings, have been either costly, time-consuming to prepare, difficult to find — or all of the above! Expense and effort are often the way we show guests the worthiness of the dishes being served.

Not so barbecue. Yet what better foods for feasting can there be than those hot off the grill, enjoyed in the company of friends in a mood of relaxation. Even the humble chicken is transformed by fire.

Chicken is a universal grill favorite because you can change its character simply by changing the marinade. There seems to be no limit to the wardrobe of flavors that chicken can wear, and this is particularly true when you start with the convenient boneless and skinless chicken breast. It is truly the chameleon of the food world.

Maple Mustard Grilled Chicken — a tribute to one of Canada's greatest natural resources, maple syrup! — is a quick-and-easy dish that should be started the night before for best flavor. No single ingredient predominates; rather, everything comes together to create a symphony of good taste.

MAPLE MUSTARD GRILLED CHICKEN

It's hard to imagine that anything this simple to make could taste so good. Serve with boiled new potatoes, grilled vegetables and mixed salad greens.

2 tbsp	PC Dijon Mustard	25 mL
3 tbsp	PC Balsamic Vinegar	45 mL
1/2 cup	PC Peanut Oil	125 mL
1/2 cup	PC 100% Pure Maple Syrup	125 mL
1 tsp	coarsely ground pepper	5 mL
1 tsp	PC Chopped Garlic in Oil	5 mL
6	PC Frozen Boneless Skinless Seasoned Chicken Breasts, thawed	6

• In small bowl, mix together mustard, vinegar, oil, maple syrup, pepper and garlic.
• Arrange chicken in shallow glass dish. Add maple syrup mixture and toss to coat.
• Cover and refrigerate at least 4 to 6 hours, preferably overnight.
• Grill chicken over medium-high heat, basting periodically with any leftover marinade, for 5 to 7 minutes per side or until no longer pink inside. Serve with boiled new potatoes and grilled mixed mushrooms.
Makes 6 servings.

PC Frozen Chicken Breasts for the Grill

Our frozen boneless chicken breasts, skinless or with the skin left on for extra crispness and flavor, are the linchpins of summer barbecues — an indispensable part of the season because you just thaw and grill.

We might not go as far as the American humorist Roy Blount Jr., who'd like to see crisp brown poultry skin be officially declared a major food group, but we appreciate how chicken skin conserves moisture and adds flavor. As with other meats, much of the flavor of chicken comes from its fat; and in chicken, much of this fat lies beneath the skin.

Even if you don't like to eat chicken skin, keep it on during cooking and remove it right after. This way, the skin gets to act as a "lid" to help keep in moisture. Studies conducted at the University of Minnesota showed that, contrary to popular belief, fat from the skin doesn't "migrate" into the flesh during cooking.

RANCHERO CHICKEN BREASTS

We call someone who tends horses and cattle a "rancher." The word evolved from the Spanish rancheros, *which itself derived from the breeding farms, or* ranchos, *that the Spanish colonizers established in the New World for the purpose of propagating their cattle and Arab and Barb strains of horses.*

6	PC Frozen Chicken Breasts for the Grill or PC Frozen Boneless Skinless Seasoned Chicken Breasts, thawed	6
2 tbsp	coarsely cracked black pepper	25 mL
1½ cups	PC Ranch Dressing	375 mL

- Wipe chicken breasts with damp cloth and pat dry.
- Using hands, pat pepper all over chicken.
- Arrange chicken in shallow glass dish. Pour ranch dressing over top and toss to coat well.
- Cover and marinate in refrigerator for 6 to 8 hours or overnight.
- On lightly greased grill over medium-high heat, cook breasts for 6 to 8 minutes per side or until chicken is no longer pink inside. Serve with Grilled Bread Salad with Roasted Red Peppers & Cherry Tomatoes (p. 220) and grilled corn on the cob.

Makes 6 servings.

PC Memories of
Montego Bay
Jerk Marinade

METAL SKEWERS
SHOULD BE FLAT-
SIDED OR TWISTED
SO THAT THE MEAT
OR VEGETABLES
DON'T SLIP AROUND
WHEN TURNING.
IF YOU PREFER
WOODEN SKEWERS,
SOAK FOR AT LEAST
30 MINUTES
BEFORE USING TO
PREVENT BURNING.

▼

Malay food is the original cuisine of the Malay Archipelago, most of which is occupied by Indonesia. And its most famous dish is *satay* (SAH-tay) — barbecued skewers of chicken, beef or mutton served with a spicy peanut sauce. Malay food, which is one of the three main cuisines of Singapore (the other two are Chinese and Indian), is not always hot, but it's always gently spiced to highly aromatic.

The word "jerk" might describe some of us when we let loose with friends, but here it's used to describe an amalgam of heat and spice. Jerk is the defining flavor of Jamaican grilled meats.

Our satay recipe is a crossover of several cuisines: Malay (the concept), Jamaican (the jerk flavors) and Indian (the cooling minted yogurt sauce). You can offer satay as an appetizer or make a meal of it. In Indonesia, satay is a popular snack that is readily available from neighborhood food hawkers.

JERK CHICKEN SATAY WITH MINTED YOGURT

For a milder dish, substitute PC Vague Memories of Montego Bay The Timid Jerk Marinade. Or use our already marinated PC Vague Memories of Montego Bay The Timid Jerk Frozen Glazed Chicken Breast Portions; just thaw, slice, skewer and grill.

8	PC Frozen Boneless Skinless Seasoned Chicken Breasts, thawed	8
1½ cups	PC Memories of Montego Bay Jerk Marinade	375 mL
1 cup	PC 'Too Good To Be True!' Fat-Free Plain Yogurt	250 mL
1 tbsp	PC Mint Sauce	15 mL
1 tsp	PC Louisiana Hot Sauce	5 mL

• Slice chicken breasts lengthwise into 3 strips. Thread strips lengthwise onto skewers. (If using wooden skewers, soak for 30 minutes before using.)

• Pour 1 cup (250 mL) Memories of Montego Bay marinade in shallow glass dish. Add skewered chicken breasts and turn to coat well. Let marinate at room temperature for 1 to 2 hours or 6 to 8 hours in the refrigerator.

• Meanwhile, in small bowl, mix together yogurt, mint sauce and Louisiana hot sauce. Chill until using.

• On lightly greased grill over medium-high heat, cook satay, turning often and brushing with remaining ½ cup (125 mL) Memories of Montego Bay marinade, for about 15 minutes or until cooked through.

• Serve with minted yogurt for dipping.

Makes 6 to 8 servings.

PC Gigantico Frozen
Seasoned Chicken
Drumsticks

NEVER THAW

CHICKEN AT ROOM

TEMPERATURE.

RATHER, THAW IN

REFRIGERATOR

OR IN COLD WATER

(IN SEALED

PACKAGES) OR IN

MICROWAVE (ON

DEFROST SETTING,

SEPARATING PIECES

AND TURNING

ALONG THE WAY).

▾

For all his bright thoughts, Socrates was a little too long on logic when it came to food. For instance, the Greek philosopher reasoned against the common use of spices and condiments as a way to stimulate the appetite and aid digestion. He much preferred the stimulating effects of jogging — quite literally! — over those little table extras like mustard or sauces. (Socrates was no slouch; he got physical long before the world heard of aerobics. At a ripe old age, he took up dancing — not for art or recreation, but for the health of it. He believed dancing promoted well-being in every part of the body.)

One day, when Socrates had nearly exhausted himself from running, a friend asked why he was expending all that effort. The philosopher retorted, "Can't you see that I am seasoning my dinner?"

Unlike Socrates, we like food with bold flavors. We also want it to involve very little physical effort. So we have high praise for this dish since it manages to achieve both. The turkey thighs and drums are our famous, meaty PC Giganticos, and they're flavored with PC Szechwan Barbecue Sauce, a gourmet barbecue sauce with a spicy peanut twist.

SZECHWAN BARBECUED CHICKEN

These Gigantico thighs and drumsticks look and taste terrific. Yet for all that, they're a cinch to make. They were trial tested for a crowd of 50 and received nothing but kudos. After our Jerk Racks of Lamb (p. 88), this may be the next easiest dish in the book.

6	PC Gigantico Frozen Seasoned Chicken Thighs, thawed	6
6	PC Gigantico Frozen Seasoned Chicken Drumsticks, thawed	6
1 tbsp	PC Spicy Barbecue Seasoning	15 mL
1 cup	PC Szechwan Barbecue Sauce	250 mL

• Season thighs and drumsticks with spicy barbecue seasoning.
• Arrange on baking sheet and roast in 375°F (190°C) oven just until flesh is no longer pink, about 35 to 40 minutes.
• Transfer chicken pieces to lightly greased grill over medium-high heat and cook, turning frequently, until skin is crisp, about 6 to 8 minutes.
• Brush all over with barbecue sauce and continue cooking, turning often, until sauce caramelizes, about 3 to 4 minutes. Serve with Grilled Red & White Potato Salad (p. 218), 5-Minute Coleslaw (p. 196) and/or 7-Bean Salad with Mint & Basil (p. 228).
Makes 6 servings.

Next to hot dogs and hamburgers, the "new" chicken salad (the one your grandmother never knew about) is one of summer's favorite offerings. Gone are the mingy pieces of white or dark meat mixed with too much mayonnaise and sprinkled with paprika. Instead, chunks of chicken breast are now flavored with soya sauce and made crunchy with broccoli; or simply dressed with *crème fraîche*, the tangy, nutty tasting cultured cream, and served on a bed of wine-red radicchio leaves.

The variations are infinite and depend on the cook and ingredients at hand. Barbecued Jerk Chicken Salad, made with PC Vague Memories of Montego Bay The Timid Jerk Glazed Chicken Breast Portions, surpassed all our expectations for a truly different chicken salad. It's spicy, but not overly, and has a good degree of crunch. We give it 5 (out of 10) on the heat scale and 12 (out of 10) for taste!

Turn the pages to find three more chicken salad favorites: Raspberry Chicken with Red & Green Cabbage Salad, Szechwan Peanut Chicken Salad and Paul's Favorite Chicken Salad.

PC Vague Memories of Montego Bay The Timid Jerk Frozen Glazed Chicken Breast Portions

BARBECUED JERK CHICKEN SALAD

If PC Vague Memories of Montego Bay The Timid Jerk Glazed Chicken Breast Portions aren't available, marinate boneless, skinless chicken breasts in 1/2 cup (125 mL) PC Vague Memories of Montego Bay The Timid Jerk Marinade for 1 to 2 hours at room temperature or 4 to 6 hours in the refrigerator.

4	PC Vague Memories of Montego Bay The Timid Jerk Frozen Glazed Chicken Breast Portions, thawed	4
3 tbsp	finely chopped red or green onion(s)	45 mL
1	stalk celery, chopped	1
1	small red bell pepper, chopped	1
3 tbsp	PC The Ultimate Mayonnaise	45 mL
2 tbsp	PC Gourmet Barbecue Sauce	25 mL
1/2 tsp	PC Louisiana Hot Sauce	2 mL
	Salt and freshly ground pepper	
1 tbsp	finely chopped parsley	15 mL

• On greased grill over medium-high heat, grill chicken for 5 to 7 minutes per side or until flesh is no longer pink. Cut into 1/2- to 1-inch (1.2 to 2.5 cm) cubes.
• Place chicken in bowl. Add onion, celery, red pepper, mayonnaise, barbecue sauce, hot sauce and salt and pepper to taste. Toss well.
• Cover and chill for 20 to 30 minutes.
• Just before serving, sprinkle with parsley.
Makes 4 servings.

THE SECRET OF A GREAT CHICKEN SALAD IS TO COOK, NOT OVERCOOK, THE CHICKEN. CHICKEN IS READY TO TAKE OFF THE GRILL WHEN IT'S TENDER AND THE FLESH IS NO LONGER PINK.

PC Frozen Boneless
Skinless Seasoned
Chicken Breasts

RASPBERRY CHICKEN WITH
RED & GREEN CABBAGE SALAD

This dish, shown above, is perfection. Everyone will be as impressed by its presentation as by its tantalizing flavors.

4	PC Frozen Boneless Skinless Seasoned Chicken Breasts, thawed	4
1/2 cup	PC The Decadent Raspberry Balsamic Vinaigrette	125 mL
1/2	red cabbage, shredded	1/2
1/2	green cabbage, shredded	1/2
2	carrots, cut in thin julienne strips	2
1/2	red onion, thinly sliced	1/2
1/2 cup	PC The Ultimate Mayonnaise	125 mL
1/2 cup	PC Memories of Gilroy Creamy Roasted Garlic Sauce	125 mL
1/4 cup	PC Seasoned Rice Vinegar	50 mL
	Salt and freshly ground pepper	

You can put everything, and the more things the better, into a salad, as into a conversation; but everything depends on the skill of mixing.

— Charles D. Warner
(1829-1900)

- Wipe chicken breasts with damp cloth and pat dry.
- Combine chicken breasts with raspberry balsamic vinaigrette and toss to coat. Cover and let marinate in refrigerator for 4 to 6 hours or, preferably, overnight.
- On lightly greased grill over medium-high heat, cook chicken for 5 to 7 minutes per side or just until flesh is no longer pink. Let cool.
- Prepare cabbage salad: Mix together red and green cabbage, carrots, red onion, mayonnaise, Memories of Gilroy sauce and rice vinegar. Season with salt and pepper to taste.
- Arrange cabbage salad on 4 individual salad plates. Slice chicken breasts and place on top.

Makes 4 servings.

TENDER BREASTS OF CHICKEN PERMEATED WITH A SPICY PEANUT SAUCE INSPIRED OUR SZECHWAN PEANUT CHICKEN SALAD, SHOWN ABOVE. SEE RECIPE NEXT PAGE.

SZECHWAN PEANUT CHICKEN SALAD

This chicken salad (pictured on preceding page) has many of the flavors found in the Indonesian dish gado-gado, *a salad plate of green beans, potatoes, hard-cooked eggs, lightly cooked cabbage wedges and bean sprouts topped with a spicy peanut sauce.*

PC Memories of
Szechwan Frozen
Chicken Breast Portions

12	small new potatoes	12
¹/₂ lb	green beans	250 g
4	PC Memories of Szechwan Frozen Chicken Breast Portions, thawed	4
4	peeled and cored rings of fresh pineapple, ¹/₂ inch (1 cm) thick	4
1	bag (175 g) PC California-Style Field Salad or 3 to 4 cups (750 mL to 1 L) mixed greens and reds of your choice	1
2 cups	bean sprouts	500 mL
1	small red onion, thinly sliced	1
¹/₂ cup	PC Unsalted Dry-Roasted Peanuts	125 mL

Spicy Yogurt Dressing:

¹/₄ cup	PC Memories of Szechwan Peanut Sauce	50 mL
¹/₄ cup	PC Memories of Bangkok Spicy Thai Sauce	50 mL
¹/₄ cup	PC 'Too Good To Be True!' Fat-Free Plain Yogurt	50 mL
1 tbsp	chopped fresh coriander	15 mL

• Cook potatoes in boiling salted water until tender, about 10 to 15 minutes. Slice in half and set aside.

• Trim green beans; steam or boil for a few minutes until tender but firm. Let cool.

• Prepare Spicy Yogurt Dressing: Mix together Memories of Szechwan sauce, Memories of Bangkok sauce, yogurt and coriander. Set aside.

• On greased grill over medium-high heat, cook chicken breasts for 5 to 7 minutes per side or just until flesh is no longer pink. About 5 minutes before chicken is done, add pineapple and potatoes to grill and cook 2 to 3 minutes per side or until heated through and lightly charred. Slice pineapple rings into quarters.

• To assemble: Arrange salad greens and reds on each of 4 individual salad plates. Arrange potatoes, green beans, bean sprouts, pineapple and red onion on top. Slice chicken into strips and add to each plate.

• Drizzle dressing over top; sprinkle with peanuts.

Makes 4 servings.

PAUL'S FAVORITE CHICKEN SALAD

Our VP of Product Development, Paul Uys, knew this salad as Coronation Salad in his native South Africa, where it is a very popular lunch and buffet dish. Apparently, it was created in 1952 to celebrate the coronation of Queen Elizabeth II. Don't overdo the PC Italian Magic tomato sauce; you need only enough to tint the dressing.

PC Over 50% Fruit French-Style Pure Apricot Jam

4	PC Frozen Boneless Skinless Seasoned Chicken Breasts, thawed	4
1 tbsp	PC Extra-Virgin Olive Oil	15 mL
1	onion, finely chopped	1
2 tbsp	PC Memories of Jaipur Curry & Passion Fruit Sauce	25 mL
2	apples, cut in ½-inch (1 cm) cubes	2
1 cup	chopped celery	250 mL
4 tbsp	dry sherry	60 mL
1 tbsp	PC Italian Magic Homestyle Italian Sauce or other tomato sauce	15 mL
1 tbsp	fresh lemon juice	15 mL
2 tbsp	PC Over 50% Fruit French-Style Pure Apricot Jam	25 mL
4 to 6 tbsp	or more PC The Ultimate Mayonnaise	60 to 90 mL
3 tbsp	whipping cream (optional)	45 mL
	Salt and freshly ground pepper	

- On greased grill over medium-high heat, cook chicken breasts for 5 to 7 minutes per side or just until flesh is no longer pink. Let cool and cut into ½- to 1-inch (1.2 to 2.5 cm) cubes.
- In skillet, heat oil. Add onion and cook, stirring often, until tender. Stir in Memories of Jaipur sauce and cook for 1 minute. Then add apples, celery, sherry, Italian Magic, lemon juice and apricot jam. Cook for 2 to 3 minutes, stirring occasionally. Remove from heat and let cool.
- Stir in chicken, mayonnaise, whipping cream, if using, and salt and pepper to taste.
- Serve immediately or refrigerate for a few hours and serve at room temperature.

Makes 4 to 6 servings.

*Mayonnaise:
One of the
sauces that serve
the French in
place of
a state religion.*

— Ambrose Bierce
(1842-1914)

A worthy summertime feast: Plump, butterflied Rock Cornish hen grilled in half the time it takes to barbecue a whole chicken. For our secret, turn the page.

PC Jalapeño
Pepper Jelly

ON THE GRILL,
YOU CAN FLATTEN A
BUTTERFLIED
CHICKEN FURTHER BY
PLACING AN
OLD BAKING SHEET
ON TOP AND
WEIGHTING IT DOWN
WITH A
COUPLE OF BRICKS.

▼

patchcocking has retained its culinary meaning of "a chicken cooked hurriedly" since medieval days. By splitting poultry down the back and flattening, a process also known as "butterflying," you can cut cooking time by nearly half. Butterflied hens take about 20 to 30 minutes to cook.

Spatchcocking is easily done at home (refer to drawings on opposite page) and is a particularly appealing way to cook Rock Cornish hens. Kept whole, there is a greater risk of overcooking the tender breast meat. Once the birds are butterflied, mix up an easy marinade-and-glaze to complement their mild flavor. The one featured here brings together three key oriental flavors — lemon, ginger and black bean — and the heat of jalapeños.

GRILLED ROCK CORNISH HENS

Some Cornish hens are plumper than others. If your guest list includes children or light eaters, calculate half a hen per person.

4	Rock Cornish hens	4
4 tbsp	PC 'Too Good To Be True!' Lemon-Herb Seasoning	60 mL
1/2 cup	PC Memories of San Francisco Golden Gate Lemon Ginger Sauce	125 mL
2 tbsp	PC Memories of Hong Kong Spicy Black Bean and Garlic Sauce	25 mL
1/2 cup	PC Jalapeño Pepper Jelly	125 mL
3 tbsp	PC Seasoned Rice Vinegar	45 mL
	Salt and freshly ground pepper	

• Using kitchen or poultry shears, cut along entire length of backbone of Cornish hens as near as possible to centre (see diagram 1, opposite page). Turn breast-side up and, with the heel of your hand, flatten birds as much as possible (diagram 2). Rub all over with lemon-herb seasoning.

• Prepare marinade: Mix together Memories of San Francisco sauce, Memories of Hong Kong sauce, jalapeño pepper jelly, rice vinegar and salt and pepper to taste.

• Brush hens all over with marinade. Cover and refrigerate for 2 to 4 hours. Let warm to room temperature before cooking.

• On greased grill over medium-high heat, cook hens for 3 to 5 minutes per side or until seared all over. Reduce heat to medium-low and continue cooking, brushing often with marinade, until juices run clear when pierced with fork, about 8 to 10 minutes per side.

Makes 4 servings.

ARPI'S GRILLED CHICKEN WITH HOT PLUM SAUCE

This superb dish comes from popular Toronto chef Arpi Magyar, of Splendido Bar & Grill. For more of Arpi's recipes, see p.145.

2	whole chickens (each about 3 lb/1.5 kg)	2
2 to 3 tbsp	PC Extra-Virgin Olive Oil	30 to 45 mL
2 tbsp.	PC Lime Cilantro Seasoning	30 mL
1/4 cup	chopped fresh thyme	50 mL
1/2 cup	(approx.) PC Memories of Canton Hot Plum Sauce	125 mL
1	large red onion, cut in 1/2-inch (1 cm) rounds	1
8	baby bok choy, cut in half	8
4	large peaches, halved and pitted	4
	Salt and freshly ground pepper	
	Chopped or torn fresh basil and coriander	

• Using kitchen or poultry shears, cut along entire length of backbone of chickens as near as possible to centre (see diagram 1, below). Invert and, with the heel of your hand, flatten birds as much as possible (diagram 2).

• Brush chickens all over with oil. Sprinkle with lime cilantro seasoning and chopped fresh thyme.

• Place chickens skin-side down on lightly oiled grill over high heat and cook for 3 to 4 minutes, then turn and cook over medium heat. Brush with some of the Memories of Canton sauce and continue cooking for 20 to 25 minutes or until juices run clear. Let rest for 10 minutes, then slice each chicken in half.

• Meanwhile, brush onion rounds, bok choy and peaches lightly with oil. Season with salt and pepper to taste. Place on grill and cook, turning often, until lightly charred, but still intact.

• On large platter, arrange chicken, bok choy, onion and peaches. Sprinkle all over with basil and coriander. Serve with remaining Memories of Canton sauce, gently heated until warm.

Makes 4 servings.

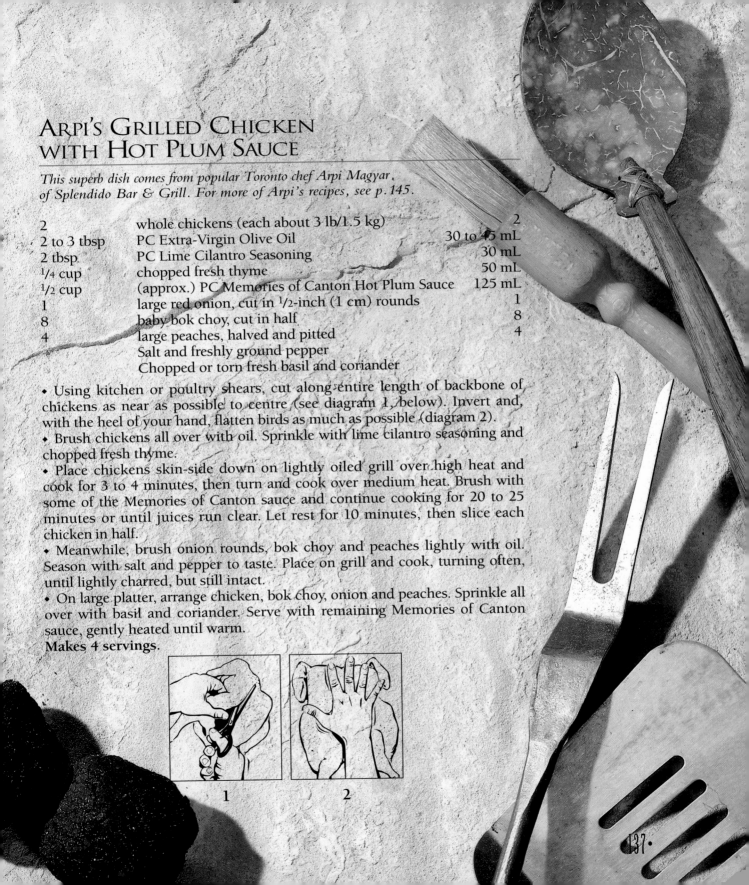

1   2

ROBERTO MARTELLA

GRANO CAFFE-FORNO · 2035 YONGE STREET · TORONTO · (416) 440-1986

SPLENDIDO PIZZA WITH GRILLED CHICKEN, MUSHROOMS & GORGONZOLA

"Eating is convivial," says Roberto Martella. And what better way could there be to express camaraderie than by sharing a pizza hot off the grill.

2	PC Frozen Boneless Skinless Seasoned Chicken Breasts, thawed	2
1/2	pkg (12 oz/336 g) PC Assorted Gourmet Mushrooms or 2 cups (500 mL) mixed mushrooms (e.g., cremini, shiitake, oyster, white)	1/2
	PC Extra-Virgin Olive Oil	
1	PC Original Splendido Italian-Style Flatbread (11 in/28 cm)	1
	PC Pure Olive Oil with Hot Pepper Essence	
3 tbsp	PC Splendido Spicy Roasted Garlic Pasta Sauce	45 mL
1/3 cup	crumbled Gorgonzola cheese	75 mL
	Salt and freshly ground pepper	

• On greased grill over medium-high heat, grill chicken for 5 to 7 minutes per side or until cooked through. Cut into thin strips.
• Clean mushrooms with brush or damp cloth. Brush with extra-virgin olive oil. Place on grill and cook until tender and lightly charred, about 8 to 10 minutes, turning halfway through. Thinly slice.
• Brush Splendido lightly with hot pepper olive oil. Place top-side down on grill and cook for a few minutes until top is golden brown.
• Spread pasta sauce over Splendido. Top with chicken and mushrooms. Add Gorgonzola cheese.
• Return pizza to grill and cook until bottom is lightly toasted. Turn off heat and cook with lid down until cheese is melted. Season with salt and freshly ground pepper to taste.
Makes 4 to 6 servings.

Classic Pizza Variation: Brush Splendido lightly with PC Roasted Garlic-Flavored Olive Oil. Place top-side down on greased grill over medium-high heat and cook for a few minutes until top is golden brown. Spread top with PC Splendido Spicy Roasted Garlic Pasta Sauce. Arrange thin slices of fresh tomato on top. Sprinkle with shredded mozzarella cheese. Add a few fresh basil leaves and sprinkle lightly with PC Gourmet Blend 100% Grated Parmesan Cheese. Return to grill and cook until bottom is lightly toasted. Turn off heat and cook with cover down until cheese is melted. Season with salt and pepper to taste.
Makes 4 to 6 servings.

THE BASICS IN LIFE ARE THE STUFF OF CULTURE, ACCORDING TO ROBERTO MARTELLA, WHO LONG AGO EMBARKED ON HIS OWN APPRENTICESHIP WITH THE CULTURES OF THE WORLD BY TRAVELLING THE GLOBE. "LEARN TO ENJOY EXPERIMENTING WITH FOODS OUTSIDE YOUR NORMAL CULTURAL MILIEU," HE SAYS. ROBERTO TAKES HIS OWN ADVICE. THE FOOD AT GRANO, HE SAYS, HAS BEEN DESCRIBED AS "ITALIAN DONE CHINESE STYLE" BECAUSE OF ITS EMPHASIS ON UNCOMPLICATED, EARTHY, YET SOPHISTICATED FLAVORS. IN THE RECIPES HERE, "WHAT YOU SEE IS WHAT YOU TASTE," SAYS ROBERTO. A RESPECT FOR THE INTRINSIC TASTE OF ONE'S INGREDIENTS IS A HALLMARK OF ALL GOOD COOKING, HE SAYS.

MARK McEWAN
NORTH 44° · 2537 YONGE STREET · TORONTO · (416) 487-4897

SMOKED CORN RISOTTO

Season the risotto well in the initial stages, Mark advises. "It's difficult to play catch-up after the dish is cooked." Mark serves this dish with grilled lamb rack (see sidebar for marinade recipe).

2	ears of corn, shucked and smoked (see method below)	2
6 cups	(approx.) chicken stock, homemade or made with PC Fresh Concentrated Chicken Stock	1.5 L
2 tbsp	PC Extra-Virgin Olive Oil	25 mL
1 tsp	PC Chopped Garlic in Oil or chopped fresh garlic	5 mL
2 to 3 tbsp	chopped fresh shallots	30 to 45 mL
1 1/2 cups	arborio rice (available in many supermarkets)	375 mL
1/2 cup	dry white wine	125 mL
	Salt and freshly ground pepper	
Pinch	nutmeg	Pinch
1	red bell pepper, roasted, peeled and finely chopped	1
2	green onions, finely chopped	2
2 to 3 tbsp	PC Memories of Reggiano Parmigiano Reggiano Caesar Dressing or freshly grated Parmesan cheese	30 to 45 mL

• To smoke corn: Sprinkle a few dampened hardwood chips onto medium-hot coals and heat until smoldering. Turn off gas and wait 1 minute for heat to dissipate. Place corn on grill; close lid and let smoke for 30 minutes. (Alternatively, cook corn on grill over medium-high heat, turning a few times, until lightly charred.) Using sharp knife, cut kernels off cobs. Set aside.

• Keep chicken stock at simmer while preparing risotto.

• Heat oil in saucepan over medium-high heat. Add garlic and shallots and cook, stirring, until tender and fragrant; do not brown. Add arborio rice and cook, stirring, for 1 minute.

• Add wine and continue cooking, stirring constantly, until most of wine is absorbed. Season well with salt, pepper and nutmeg.

• Add chicken stock, 1/2 cup (125 mL) at a time, stirring constantly and waiting until most of liquid is absorbed before adding next instalment. Continue in this manner until rice is tender but slightly resistant to the bite, about 18 to 22 minutes; with second last addition of stock, add corn kernels, chopped red pepper and green onions.

• Stir in Memories of Reggiano sauce or freshly grated Parmesan cheese. Taste and adjust seasoning.

Makes 4 to 6 servings.

MARK McEWAN SERVES THIS SENSATIONAL RISOTTO WITH GRILLED RACK OF LAMB. "THEY COOK IN ABOUT THE SAME AMOUNT OF TIME, SO YOU CAN BRING THIS DINNER TOGETHER QUICKLY," SAYS THE CHEF AND PROPRIETOR OF NORTH 44°. "EVEN IF YOU DON'T HAVE A SIDE BURNER, YOU CAN COOK THE RISOTTO ON ONE SIDE OF THE GRILL AND LAMB ON THE OTHER." MARK SUGGESTS MARINATING 4 LAMB RACKS FOR 1 HOUR IN A MIXTURE OF 1/2 CUP (125 mL) PC HOT RED PEPPER JELLY, 2 TBSP (25 mL) PC BALSAMIC VINEGAR, 2 TSP (10 mL) PC CHOPPED GARLIC IN OIL AND 1 TSP (5 mL) PC LIME CILANTRO SEASONING.

Arpi Magyar

Splendido Bar & Grill · 88 Harbord Street · Toronto · (416) 929-7788

GRILLED STRIP LOIN PEPPER STEAKS

These flavorful steaks take only a few minutes to make.

| 4 to 6 | PC Memories of Lyon Frozen Marinated Boneless Strip Loin Pepper Steaks, thawed PC Pure Olive Oil with Lemon Essence | 4 to 6 |

• Brush steaks all over with oil. Place on lightly greased grill over high heat and cook for 2 to 3 minutes per side or to desired doneness.
Makes 4 to 6 servings.

COUSCOUS WITH MINT

A superb blend of flavors in one easy salad. Serve warm or at room temperature.

2¹/2 cups	chicken stock, homemade or made with PC Fresh Concentrated Chicken Stock	625 mL
2 cups	PC Memories of Marrakech Couscous	500 mL
1 tbsp	each grated orange and lime rind	15 mL
2 tbsp	finely chopped onion	25 mL
1/4 cup	chopped fresh mint	50 mL
2 tsp	each cumin and turmeric	10 mL
Pinch	cinnamon	Pinch
2 tbsp	PC Pure Olive Oil with Lemon Essence	25 mL
2 tbsp	fresh lemon juice	25 mL

• Bring chicken stock to boil. Stir in couscous, cover and remove from heat.
• Combine with orange and lime rind, onion, mint, cumin, turmeric, cinnamon, olive oil and lemon juice. Mix well.
Makes 4 to 6 servings.

CORN SALSA

A quick-and-easy accompaniment to the grilled pepper steaks.

3	ears of corn, shucked Juice of 1/2 lemon	3
3 tbsp	each chopped fresh parsley and red onion	45 mL
4 to 6	PC Splendido Sun-Dried Tomatoes, thinly sliced	4 to 6
2 tbsp	PC Memories of Sonoma Dried Tomato Sauce Salt and freshly ground pepper	30 mL

• Grill corn until tender and lightly charred; cut off kernels. Combine with lemon juice, parsley, red onion, sun-dried tomatoes and Memories of Sonoma sauce. Mix well. Season with salt and pepper.
Makes 4 to 6 servings.

ELENA EMBRIONI

SOUTHERN ACCENT · 595 MARKHAM STREET · TORONTO · (416) 536-3211

Hot & Spicy Grilled Ribs
with Banana Barbecue Sauce

Elena serves these ribs with a spicy bean salad: Mix together 1 jar (28 oz/796 mL) PC 'Too Good To Be True!' 7 Bean Mix, rinsed and drained, and 2 to 3 tbsp (30 to 45 mL) each chopped red bell pepper, chopped green onion, chopped red onion and chopped fresh cilantro. Dress with 1 tbsp (15 mL) each PC Pure Olive Oil with Hot Pepper Essence and PC Balsamic Vinegar. Season with salt and pepper to taste.

4	racks pork back ribs (each about 1½ lb/750 g)	4
2 cups	PC Memories of Thailand Fiery Thai Dipping Sauce	500 mL
2 to 3	slices PC Naturally Smoked Bacon, chopped	2 to 3
1 tbsp	PC Chopped Garlic in Oil	15 mL
1 to 2 tbsp	PC Puréed Ginger	15 to 30 mL
⅓ cup	PC 'Too Good To Be True!' Twice The Fruit 3 Fruit Ultra Light Marmalade Type Spread	75 mL
1 cup	ketchup-style chili sauce	250 mL
2 to 3	bananas, thinly sliced (reserve a few slices for garnish)	2 to 3
1 tsp	dried red pepper flakes (optional)	5 mL
	Salt and freshly ground pepper	
4 to 6	collard greens, rinsed and patted dry	4 to 6
	PC Pure Olive Oil with Hot Pepper Essence	

• Place ribs in large shallow dish. Add 1½ cups (375 mL) Memories of Thailand sauce and turn to coat. Cover and let marinate in refrigerator for 24 hours. Let return to room temperature before cooking.

• Place ribs on greased grill over medium-high heat, reserving marinade. Cook, turning and brushing with reserved marinade, until crispy and slightly charred, about 20 to 30 minutes.

• Meanwhile, in saucepan over medium-high heat, cook bacon for 2 to 3 minutes or until golden brown. Add garlic and ginger and cook, stirring, until fragrant. Stir in 3 Fruit spread, chili sauce, ½ cup (125 mL) Memories of Thailand sauce, bananas, red pepper flakes (if using) and salt and pepper to taste. Bring to boil, reduce heat and let simmer, stirring frequently, for about 15 to 20 minutes.

• Just before ribs are done, place collard greens on grill and brush lightly with hot pepper oil. Cook about 1 minute or until they turn vivid green and start to wilt, then turn and cook about 1 minute more.

• Place a collard green on each plate and top with rack of ribs. Spoon banana barbecue sauce on top. Serve with bean salad on the side. Garnish with a few slices of banana.

Makes 4 servings.

ARGENTINIAN-BORN ELENA EMBRIONI COMES FROM THE LAND OF CHIMICHURRI — A HOT AND SPICY MARINADE ENLIVENED WITH GARLIC AND HOT PEPPERS — SO CAJUN AND CREOLE COOKING HAS BEEN AN EASY TRANSITION FOR HER. FOR THIS MENU, THE CHEF OF SOUTHERN ACCENT HAS CHOSEN DISHES THAT ARE FULL OF HEAT AND FLAVOR. "I NEED TO HAVE MY RIBS REALLY HOT," SHE SAYS, ADDING THAT SHE NEVER PRECOOKS THEM. "IT'S NOT NECESSARY. I PREFER TO MARINATE THEM OVERNIGHT IN A SPICY SAUCE. IF THE RIBS ARE GOOD, THE ACID IN YOUR SAUCE WILL TENDERIZE THE MEAT. I ALWAYS RECOMMEND THAT PEOPLE MARINATE RIB MEAT, EVEN IF IT'S ONLY WITH FRESH LEMON JUICE."

ALBINO SILVA
CHIADO · 864 COLLEGE STREET · TORONTO · (416) 538-1910

PORK LOIN WITH GRILLED APPLES

"We had citrus trees in Portugal and used them continually," says Albino Silva. "Pork was always available and as soon as it came off the grill, we squeezed a little fresh orange juice over it." This dish incorporates the flavors of Albino's homeland.

1	PC Frozen Danish Pork Loin (4 to 5 lb/2 to 2.5 kg), thawed	1
5	apples, cored (e.g., Royal Gala, Golden Delicious)	5
4 tbsp	PC Over 50% Fruit Pure Seville Orange Marmalade	60 mL
4 tbsp	PC Jumbo Raisins	60 mL
	Salt and pepper (freshly ground and coarsely cracked)	
1 tbsp	PC Chopped Garlic in Oil	15 mL
5 tbsp	PC Premium Alfalfa Honey	75 mL
2 tbsp	PC Dijon Mustard	30 mL
1/3 cup	PC Memories of Bangkok Spicy Thai Sauce	75 mL
3 tbsp	Port wine	45 mL
2	onions, halved through core and cut in wedges	2
2 tbsp	PC Extra-Virgin Olive Oil	30 mL
2 tbsp	PC Aged White Wine Vinegar	30 mL

• Cut pork loin in half crosswise. Using sharp knife or the handle of a wooden spoon, create a tunnel through centre of pork loin for stuffing.

• Peel and finely chop 2 of the apples. Combine with marmalade and raisins. Using your fingers, force apple mixture into each loin. Season with salt and freshly ground pepper to taste.

• Prepare glaze: Mix together garlic, 2 tbsp (30 mL) honey, mustard, Memories of Bangkok sauce and 1 tbsp (15 mL) coarsely cracked pepper. Set glaze aside.

• Centre remaining 3 apples on 3 squares of foil large enough to wrap loosely around apples. Spoon into each hollowed out centre 1 tbsp (15 mL) each honey and port. Fold up foil loosely around apples, sealing tightly.

• Place pork loins on greased grill over high heat and cook until seared all over, about 3 to 5 minutes per side. Reduce heat to medium, add foil-wrapped apples to grill, and cook pork and apples with lid down until apples are tender and pork reaches an internal temperature of 150°F (65°C), about 40 to 50 minutes; while pork is cooking, turn and brush often with glaze.

• Let pork rest for 10 to 15 minutes. Keep apples in foil. Meanwhile, grill onion wedges for 10 minutes or until lightly charred all over. In heavy saucepan on side burner or directly on grill, heat oil and vinegar. Add onion wedges and cook for 5 minutes or until tender, stirring once or twice. Season with salt and pepper to taste.

• Slice pork and place 1 or 2 slices on each plate along with half of a grilled apple and a few grilled onion wedges.

Makes 4 to 6 servings.

CHIADO (SHEE-AH-DOE) IS BOTH THE NAME OF A FAMOUS 15TH CENTURY PORTUGUESE POET AND LISBON'S FASHIONABLE SHOPPING DISTRICT. ALBINO SILVA SPENT HIS YOUTH IN LISBON, EXCEPT FROM AGES 5 TO 9, WHEN HIS FAMILY MOVED TO THE PROVINCE OF TRAS-OS-MONTES — IT MEANS "BEHIND THE MOUNTAINS" — TO WORK A FARM-CUM-VINEYARD. "THE BEST COOKING EXPERIENCE I EVER HAD CAME FROM THAT TIME," SAYS ALBINO. "I COOKED IN ONE OF THOSE THREE-LEGGED, CAST-IRON POTS OVER AN OPEN FIRE IN THE KITCHEN. THE STONE OVEN TOOK TWO HOURS TO HEAT! SINCE THERE WERE NO FRIDGES OR FREEZERS, EVERY INGREDIENT HAD TO BE PURCHASED FRESH DAILY. I'VE COME BACK TO RUSTIC COOKING AT THE RESTAURANT."

SUZANNE BABY

LAKES BAR & GRILL · 1112 YONGE STREET · TORONTO · (416) 966-0815

GRILLED SHRIMP WITH
GAZPACHO SALAD & GARLIC BREADSTICKS

"Lemon juice softens onions and brings out their sweetness," says Suzanne Baby.

2	red onions, very thinly sliced	2
1/2 cup	(approx.) fresh lemon juice	125 mL
16	PC Zipper Back Raw Shell-On Colossal Black Tiger Shrimp (13 to 20 count), thawed	16
2 tbsp	(approx.) PC Pure Olive Oil with Hot Pepper Essence	30 mL
1 tbsp	(approx.) PC Lime Cilantro Seasoning	15 mL
1/4 cup	PC Aged Red Wine Vinegar	50 mL
1/4 cup	chopped fresh coriander (optional)	50 mL
Dash	PC 'Too Good To Be True' Light Worcestershire Sauce	Dash
Dash	PC Louisiana Hot Sauce	Dash
	Salt and freshly ground pepper	
3	ripe beefsteak tomatoes, thinly sliced	3
1	cucumber, peeled and finely chopped	1
1	each red and yellow bell pepper, finely chopped	1
1/2	stalk celery, finely chopped	1/2
1	PC Original Splendido Italian-Style Flatbread (11 in/28 cm)	1
	PC Roasted Garlic-Flavored Olive Oil	

• Marinate red onions in 3 tbsp (45 mL) lemon juice for 1 hour.

• Remove shells from shrimp, leaving tails intact. Brush with hot pepper oil. Sprinkle with lime cilantro seasoning. Set aside.

• Prepare dressing: Mix together 1/3 cup (75 mL) lemon juice, vinegar, coriander (if using), Worcestershire sauce, hot sauce and salt and pepper to taste. Set aside.

• On individual plates, arrange tomato slices, slightly overlapping, in a circle, using about 5 or 6 slices per plate. Place marinated onions in centre.

• Combine cucumber, red and yellow peppers and celery. Toss with some of dressing to lightly coat. Spoon remaining dressing over tomatoes and onions on plates. Spoon cucumber mixture on top of onions.

• Cut Splendido in half, then cut halves into strips ("breadsticks"), each 1 1/2 inches (3.5 cm) wide. Brush lightly with roasted garlic-flavored oil.

• Place shrimp and breadsticks on greased grill over medium-high heat. Cook shrimp for 1 1/2 to 2 minutes per side or just until opaque, turning when the pinkness comes through to centre; do not overcook. Cook breadsticks, turning, for 1 to 2 minutes or until crisp and lightly charred.

• Arrange 4 shrimp on top of tomatoes in ring around gazpacho salad. Arrange 2 or 3 breadsticks on plate and serve.

Makes 4 servings.

MARC THUET

CENTRO GRILL AND WINE BAR · 2472 YONGE STREET · TORONTO · (416) 483-2211

CHICKEN WITH SAUSAGE & VEGETABLES

"Offer some grilled PC Rustico bread and PC Hummus to your guests when they arrive so they can be patient waiting for the main course," suggests Marc Thuet.

4	PC Frozen Chicken Breasts for the Grill or PC Frozen Boneless Skinless Seasoned Chicken Breasts, thawed PC Roasted Garlic-Flavored Olive Oil PC 4-Peppercorn Steak Spice	4
1	pkg (12 oz/336 g) PC Assorted Fresh Gourmet Mushrooms	1
2	small zucchini, quartered lengthwise	2
1	each red and yellow bell pepper, cut in 8 wedges	1
1	Vidalia or red onion, cut crosswise in 1/2-inch (1 cm) rounds	1
2	ears of corn, shucked and cut in 1-inch (2.5 cm) rounds Salt and freshly ground pepper	2
4	PC Italian Sausages, hot or mild PC Sweet & Sour Jerk Barbecue Sauce	4
1 to 2 tbsp	PC Balsamic Vinegar	15 to 30 mL
4	PC Sun-Dried Tomatoes, plumped in hot water for 15 minutes and slivered (optional)	4
4	thin lemon slices Fresh basil leaves	4

• Brush chicken breasts with garlic-flavored olive oil and season with 4-peppercorn steak spice. Set aside.
• Brush mushrooms, zucchini, red and yellow peppers, onion and corn with garlic-flavored olive oil. Season with salt and pepper to taste.
• Place chicken, Italian sausages and vegetables on greased grill over medium-high heat. Cook chicken and sausages for 6 to 8 minutes or until chicken is cooked through and sausages are nicely browned all over. Just before removing chicken from grill, brush with jerk barbecue sauce. Cook vegetables until tender and nicely charred, turning often to prevent burning.
• Transfer grilled vegetables to large bowl. Toss with 1 tbsp (15 mL) garlic-flavored oil and balsamic vinegar. Add sun-dried tomatoes (if using).
• Leave sausages whole or cut diagonally into 3 or 4 slices.
• Arrange vegetables attractively around edge of individual plates. Place chicken breast and sausage in centre. Garnish with lemon and basil.
Makes 4 servings.

"AS YOU CAN SEE, PC PRODUCTS ALLOW YOU TO TRAVEL WITHOUT LEAVING YOUR HOME," SAYS MARC THUET, EXECUTIVE CHEF AND PART OWNER OF CENTRO. "I LOVE THE SOURNESS, SWEETNESS AND SPICE OF THE JERK SAUCE WITH THE CHICKEN. GRILLED VEGETABLES PROVIDE THE COLOR AND FLAVOR AND THEY COMPLEMENT THE CHICKEN AND SAUSAGE. WHAT I FIND VERY IMPORTANT WHEN BARBECUING IS THAT YOU MIX THE VEGETABLES WITH A LITTLE OLIVE OIL SO THEY DON'T STICK TO THE GRILL." AND IF CHICKEN BREASTS HAVE THE SKIN ON, START THEM SKIN-SIDE DOWN. "IT'S A LITTLE SECRET," HE ADDS.

MASSIMO CAPRA

PREGO DELLA PIAZZA · 150 BLOOR STREET WEST · TORONTO · (416) 920-9900

STICKBURGERS

In Morocco, meat kebabs shaped like these are called kefta *and are made of ground lamb. "The 4-Peppercorn spice eliminates the need for salt," says Massimo.*

2 lb	lean ground beef	1 kg
1/2	small onion, finely chopped	1/2
1/2	stalk celery, finely chopped	1/2
1 tbsp	finely chopped parsley	15 mL
1 tbsp	PC 4-Peppercorn Steak Spice	15 mL
2 tbsp	PC Memories of Kobe "The 2 Minute Miracle" Tamari Garlic Marinade	25 mL
4 to 6	medium-size portobello mushrooms, stems removed	4 to 6
1	large red onion, cut crosswise in 1/2-inch (1 cm) slices	1
	PC Extra-Virgin Olive Oil	
	Salt and freshly ground pepper	
1	PC Original Splendido Italian-Style Flatbread (11 in/28 cm), cut in 6 to 8 wedges	1
1	head radicchio, sliced or torn in bite-size pieces	1
4 to 6	thick slices of ripe beefsteak tomato	4 to 6
	PC Memories of Reggiano Parmigiano Reggiano Caesar Dressing	

• If using wooden skewers, soak in water for 30 minutes.

• Mix together meat, onion, celery, parsley, 4-peppercorn steak spice and Memories of Kobe marinade.

• Moisten hands with water. Take a handful of meat and mould mixture around skewers to form elongated "sausages" about 4 inches (10 cm) long and 1¼ inches (3 cm) in diameter. They should be thicker in the middle and tapered at the ends. Set aside.

• Lightly brush portobello mushrooms and onion slices with oil; season with salt and pepper to taste.

• Put stickburgers, mushrooms and onion on lightly greased grill over medium-high heat and cook for 4 to 6 minutes or until meat is done to your liking and vegetables are tender and lightly charred. Just before food is finished cooking, add Splendido wedges to grill and cook for about 1 minute until heated through and lightly charred.

• Arrange some of radicchio on one side of each plate. Place a tomato slice in centre of plate. Top tomato with a whole mushroom and onion slice. Set 1 or 2 stickburgers over vegetables. Add 1 or 2 Splendido wedges.

• Drizzle radicchio with Memories of Reggiano sauce.

Makes 4 to 6 servings.

RENÉE FOOTE
MESSIS · 97 HARBORD STREET · TORONTO · (416) 920-2186

JERK RED SNAPPER WITH CHARRED TOMATO & PEAR SALSA

"If you prefer less heat, use The Timid Jerk Marinade," advises Renée.

4 to 6	red snapper fillets, skin on	4 to 6
1/2 cup	PC Memories of Montego Bay Jerk Marinade	125 mL
2	large tomatoes, cut in half crosswise	2
1	large red onion, cut in half crosswise	1
	PC Pure Olive Oil with Lemon Essence	
2	large ripe pears, peeled and diced	2
3	green onions, diagonally sliced	3
2 to 3 tbsp	each chopped fresh basil, mint and coriander	30 to 45 mL
2 tbsp	PC Premium Alfalfa Honey	30 mL
2 tbsp	PC Aged Red Wine Vinegar	30 mL
	Salt and freshly ground pepper	
1	pkg (227 g) fresh PC Sugar Snap Peas	1
1	large red bell pepper, coarsely chopped	1
1 tbsp	PC 'Too Good To Be True!' Lemon-Herb Seasoning	15 mL
2	potatoes, cut in 1/4-inch (5 mm) slices	2
1	large bulb fennel, trimmed of woody stalks and cut through core in 1/2-inch (1 cm) slices	1

- Make 3 or 4 shallow crisscross cuts in skin side of fillets. Brush all over with Memories of Montego Bay marinade and let marinate for 30 minutes.
- Prepare salsa: Brush tomato and onion halves with oil. Place cut-side down on greased grill over medium-high heat and cook, turning, until well charred, about 6 to 8 minutes. Coarsely chop and mix with pears, green onions, basil, mint, coriander, honey, vinegar and salt and pepper to taste. Set aside.
- Tear off square piece of foil. Put sugar snap peas and red pepper in centre. Sprinkle with lemon-herb seasoning and drizzle lightly with oil. Fold edges to form well sealed packet. Set aside. Toss potato and fennel with 1 tbsp (15 mL) oil and salt and pepper to taste.
- Place foil packet, potatoes and fennel on grill over medium-high heat and cook for 10 to 12 minutes or until tender. Potatoes and fennel should be turned periodically to avoid burning; cook until lightly charred. Halfway through cooking time, add fish to grill and cook for 3 to 4 minutes per side or until cooked through.
- To assemble, put 4 or 5 slices potato and 1 slice fennel on each plate. Top with sugar snap peas and red pepper (open foil packet carefully as steam is extremely hot). Place fish on top and garnish with salsa.

Makes 4 to 6 servings.

MICHAEL BONACINI

Jump Café & Bar · Commerce Court East · Toronto · (416) 363-3400

JERK CHICKEN SANDWICH

Chef Michael Bonacini suggests varying the filling by using PC Italian-style sausages and PC Italian-Style Salsa — "or any other fun and interesting combinations you feel work well together."

4	PC Vague Memories of The Timid Jerk Frozen Glazed Chicken Breast Portions, thawed	4
4	slices red onion (about ¼ inch/5 mm thick)	4
2	ripe tomatoes, cut in half crosswise	2
	PC Pure Olive Oil with Lemon Essence	
	PC 'Too Good To Be True!' Lemon-Herb Seasoning	
1	pkg (340 g) PC Memories of Kashmir Naan Butter Bread	1
1	bag (175 g) PC California-Style Field Salad or 3 to 4 cups (750 mL to 1 L) mixed greens and reds of your choice	1
2 tbsp	PC Extra-Virgin Olive Oil	30 mL
1 tbsp	PC Seasoned Rice Vinegar	15 mL
1	container (227 g) PC Baba Ghanouj Roasted Eggplant Dip and Spread	1
8	thin slices ripe tomato	8
1	head radicchio, separated in leaves	1

♦ On greased grill over high heat, cook chicken for 5 to 7 minutes per side or until cooked through, turning periodically.

♦ Meanwhile, brush onion and tomatoes all over with lemon-flavored oil and sprinkle with lemon-herb seasoning. Add to grill and cook, turning, until heated through and lightly charred, about 3 to 5 minutes.

♦ Shortly before chicken and vegetables are done, brush Naan bread with lemon-flavored oil and place on grill for about 1 minute or until heated through and lightly charred.

♦ Toss salad greens with extra-virgin olive oil and rice vinegar. Season with lemon-herb seasoning to taste.

♦ Cut each chicken breast crosswise into 3 diagonal slices.

♦ To assemble: Spread top of each Naan bread with 2 tbsp (30 mL) baba ghanouj. On left half, place some of salad mixture and 2 thin slices tomato. Top with chicken slices. Fold right side of bread over filling and secure with toothpicks.

♦ Place sandwiches on individual plates. Garnish each with a radicchio leaf and grilled tomato half. Place a grilled onion slice over each tomato and top with a generous spoonful of baba ghanouj.

Makes 4 servings.

"I DON'T THINK WE SHOULD STOP AT STEAKS, CHOPS AND BURGERS FOR BARBECUES," SAYS MICHAEL BONACINI, CHEF AND CO-OWNER OF JUMP CAFÉ. "WE CAN DO MORE THAN THOSE TRADITIONAL DISHES. AND WHEN IT'S QUICK AND EASY TO PREPARE A WONDERFUL, TASTY MEAL, EVERYONE BENEFITS." MICHAEL'S UNUSUALLY DELICIOUS AND FAST (10 MINUTES TOPS!) JERK CHICKEN SANDWICH IS SURE TO BECOME A SUMMERTIME FAVORITE. HE CALLS IT A "LUNCHTIME POWER SNACK," BUT IT'S SATISFYING ENOUGH TO CONSTITUTE A MEAL.

FISH &
SEAFOOD

Top 10 Fish for the Grill

Fish with substance — that is, fish with dense firm flesh — is always the best choice for barbecuing. Choose the freshest fish possible and cook it the same day you buy it. Fresh fish will not smell fishy: The gills will be bright red and the flesh will be firm and spring back when touched. Whole fish will have clear eyes and shiny, bright scales. Fish fillets and steaks should be of similar size so they cook evenly.

If you must store fish, do so no longer than one day and be sure to keep it extra cold. Set it on a bed of ice or put it in the coldest part of the refrigerator.

Properly handled frozen fish that has been quick-frozen on the fishing vessel can be just as good as fresh. Frozen fish, whole or in fillets, is best thawed slowly in the refrigerator to the point where it is pliable, but still icy cold (with visible ice crystals). Allow about 10 to 12 hours per pound.

Here are your best bets; they're not ranked in any particular order of preference since all rate a "10" on our flavor scale.

• **Tuna:** This dense, steak-like fish is red when raw but turns white when cooked. When grilled, its flavor is superb. The natural oils in this fish make it self-basting.

• **Salmon:** Farmed coho and pink salmon from British Columbia are excellent grilled whole, as is Atlantic salmon from fish farms in the Bay of Fundy. The firm fatty flesh holds up well to heat since the natural oils keep the fish from drying out. Arctic char substitutes easily.

• **Swordfish:** Like tuna, swordfish is excellent for grilling, although it benefits from a marinade to keep it from drying out. It's so meaty in texture that it's sometimes called the "filet mignon of the marine world."

• **Halibut:** White and succulent, halibut's moist firm flesh is perfectly suited to grilling. You know the fish is done cooking when its flesh starts to come apart in sections.

• **Monkfish:** Called "poor man's lobster" because of its lobster meat-like texture, monkfish is virtually guaranteed not to fall apart on the grill. It's also good cut into scallop-size chunks and skewered.

• **Sea Bass:** Black sea bass is a succulent, medium dense fish with a mild flavor — fabulous grilled whole. When cooked, the meat separates into firm flakes that resemble tender white chicken and the backbone comes away like a dream; there aren't any small bones to worry about.

Chilean sea bass, which is much more readily available, isn't actually a true sea bass but a Patagonian toothfish. Fillets from this big, slow-growing fish are justifiably popular — the pristine white flesh has a mild flavor and semi-silky texture.

- **Shark** (mako or black tip): Mako shark rivals swordfish in taste and texture. Black tip is denser and has a slightly stronger flavor. Both are great as steaks or cut into chunks for fish kebabs.
- **Marlin:** Consider it a high-quality, lower-cost alternative to swordfish, which it resembles in taste and texture. Like swordfish, marlin benefits from an oil-based marinade.
- **Trout:** Whole 1- to 2-lb (500 g to 1 kg) rainbow trout are easy to handle on the grill — the skin keeps the flesh moist — as are rainbow trout fillets. Both are extremely popular, firm-fleshed favorites.
- **Snapper:** This is a mild-flavored, moderately firm fish with a loyal following. Choose either whole Atlantic red snapper or the milder tasting snapper fillets from British Columbia (they're two different species).

TIMING IS EVERYTHING

Proper timing means the difference between a great fish dinner or a disaster (we assume you have started with the best possible product). To this end, small fish and fillets are best grilled over a very hot fire on an open grill so that you can keep an eye on them. For whole fish weighing more than 3 pounds (1.5 kg) — for example, whitefish and some salmon varieties — or very thick fish fillets and steaks, cook covered. Closing the lid allows the barbecue to act like an oven, which gives the fish a chance to cook through before the skin gets too charred.

The rule about cooking fish until it flakes is not foolproof and, in fact, can result in overcooked fish. Instead, measure the fish at its thickest point and allow 10 minutes cooking time per inch (2.5 cm) — a reliable system devised some years ago by Canada's Department of Fisheries after intensive testing. (Other countries call it The Canadian Rule!) To double-check, insert the tip of a knife into the fish at the thickest part; if there's no flesh clinging to the bones or you can see a thin line of translucence in the middle, the fish is ready (residual heat will complete the cooking). Fish is safe to eat when the internal temperature is 140°F (60°C).

Cedar-scented
Plank-Grilled
Salmon: A heritage
dish reinvented
for the '90s. Turn
page for recipe.

PC Extra-Virgin
Olive Oil

Barbecue is a social event, a gastronomic potlatch similar to the ceremonial feasts practised by Pacific Coast tribes. At a potlatch (the word comes from the Nootka expression *patshatl*, which means "giving"), the host is unstinting in his hospitality. At one spectacular Kwakiutl potlatch in the early part of this century, the host not only fed several hundred guests during a two-week-long ceremony, but he also distributed among them 18,000 blankets, 700 carved silver bracelets, a dozen canoes, sewing machines, outboard motors, pots and pans, clothing, hundreds of sacks of flour, sugar, fruit and a large amount of cash!

We don't know what the guests ate during that particular potlatch, but Plank-Grilled Salmon would have made a lavish presentation for a people who knew their fish. It has been said of the Pacific Northwest Indians that "three-quarters of their food was fish and shellfish, and three-quarters of that three-quarters was salmon." And cooking salmon on cedar, alder or driftwood is the traditional technique used by the Indians for cooking and smoking their fresh catches. They would split open a salmon, flatten it, then tie it to a board set by the fire, or sandwich it between two pieces of wood and set the packet in the embers. As it cooked, the salmon would absorb the flavors of the wood.

In our '90s version, salmon is cooked on cedar planks set directly on the grill. It's a simple, foolproof way to produce moist, flavorful fillets. You never have to turn the fish or worry about burning it! All you have to do is keep an eye on the barbecue and spray the wood with water if it smokes too heavily or starts to flame. Your guests will be tantalized by the crackling sounds and the delicious aromas.

BUYING CEDAR

When you go to buy the cedar for our recipe, specify construction grade, "1-by-8" or "1-by-10." This will give you a thickness of about 3/4 inch (2 cm) and a width of 8 or 10 inches (20 or 25 cm). (Call first; not all stores carry these widths.) Ask the store to cut the cedar for you into 10- to 12-inch (25 to 30 cm) lengths. You don't have to buy the entire board — most places will sell you one or two pieces, but you may wish to buy several because this is a dish you'll want to make often!

PLANK-GRILLED SALMON

The woodsy flavor that cedar imparts to salmon is nothing short of sensational. To prepare four fillets, use one piece of well-soaked cedar, about 8 x 10 x 3/4 inch(es) (20 x 25 x 2 cm). See opposite page for information on buying cedar.

4	salmon fillets, each about 6 oz (180 g) and about 1 inch (2.5 cm) thick	4
4 tbsp	PC Extra-Virgin Olive Oil or PC Roasted Garlic-Flavored Olive Oil	60 mL
4 tbsp	finely chopped shallots or red onion	60 mL
	Coarsely crushed black peppercorns	
	Coarsely crushed pink peppercorns (optional)	
	Fresh dill sprigs	
1	lemon, cut in half	1
	Coarse salt	

• Soak overnight in water a plank of cedar large enough to hold 4 salmon fillets, roughly 8 x 10 inches (20 x 25 cm). Weight down with one or two cans of food to keep wood submerged.

• Preheat grill to high.

• Rub 4 salmon fillets all over with PC Extra-Virgin Olive Oil or PC Roasted Garlic-Flavored Olive Oil. Top salmon with a light sprinkling of finely chopped shallots or red onion and coarsely crushed black peppercorns. If desired, add coarsely crushed pink peppercorns as well.

• Top each fillet with a few sprigs of fresh dill and squeeze a little fresh lemon juice over all.

• Place plank on grill and sprinkle lightly with coarse salt. Heat with cover down for 2 to 3 minutes or just until the top of the plank is nearly dry (indicating that it's very hot). Caution: Keep a spray bottle nearby to douse flames in the event that wood starts to burn.

• Place salmon fillets on top of cedar. If you have two burners on your grill, turn one off and place salmon on that side; alternatively, if you have one burner, turn heat to lowest setting.

• Cook salmon with cover down for about 10 to 12 minutes or just until cooked nearly all the way through.

• Squeeze a little fresh lemon over salmon and serve.

Makes 4 servings.

YOU MAY COME ACROSS 1/2-INCH-THICK (1.2 CM) CEDAR BOARD. THIS THICKNESS IMPARTS A MORE INTENSE CEDAR FLAVOR TO FOOD BUT, UNFORTUNATELY, IT BURNS MORE EASILY THAN THE 3/4-INCH-THICK WOOD. IF YOU USE THE THINNER BOARD, BE SURE TO STAY CLOSE TO THE GRILL WITH A SPRAY BOTTLE OF WATER THROUGHOUT THE COOKING PROCESS.

PC All-Natural Light
(1% M.F.) Plain Yogurt

ROASTED
RED PEPPERS

PLACE WHOLE PEPPERS
ON GRILL OVER HIGH
HEAT AND COOK, TURNING
OFTEN, UNTIL WELL
CHARRED ALL OVER.
TRANSFER TO PLASTIC
BAG, SEAL WELL AND
LET SWEAT FOR ABOUT
10 MINUTES. REMOVE
STEM END AND PEEL OFF
CHARRED SKINS.
TIP: DO A FEW EXTRA,
AS THEY WILL KEEP
IN THE REFRIGERATOR
FOR 2 TO 3 DAYS.

Humans must be born with a "festival" gene because for virtually every activity imaginable, someone somewhere has organized a festival. In some cases, you have to wonder just who that someone might be!

For example, what mind conceived the Buzzard Day Festival in Hinckley, Ohio, so that people could celebrate the annual return of turkey buzzards. Or, even more flummoxing, who in Siberia proposed the annual Mosquito Festival, an occasion for attendees to seek assurances from the One On High that His little winged ones won't proliferate too much.

Conspicuous by its very absence, however, is a Canadian Salmon Festival, as barbecued salmon is surely one of this country's most enduring food rituals. In several Indian languages of the Pacific Northwest, the word for "salmon" is also the word for "fish."

In this recipe, salmon holds its own against stronger ingredients such as rosemary and garlic, which enhance but don't overwhelm the fish.

GRILLED SALMON FILLETS WITH ROASTED RED PEPPER SAUCE

Try to get the thicker, centre-cut fillets for this dish rather than the thinner, tail-end pieces. The light, flavorful sauce is quick and easy to make.

4	salmon fillets, each about 1 inch (2.5 cm) thick	4
	PC Roasted Garlic-Flavored Olive Oil	
2	cloves PC Fresh Peeled Garlic, finely chopped	2
3 to 4 tbsp	chopped fresh rosemary	45 to 60 mL
	Salt	
1	red bell pepper, roasted, peeled and coarsely chopped (see sidebar)	1
2 tbsp	PC All-Natural Light (1% M.F.) Plain Yogurt or PC 'Too Good To Be True!' Low-Fat Sour Cream Product	25 mL
1 tsp	PC Seasoned Rice Vinegar or fresh lemon juice	5 mL
	Freshly ground pepper	

• Brush salmon all over with garlic-flavored olive oil. Season with garlic, rosemary and a little salt to taste. Cover loosely and set aside.

• Place red pepper in food processor or blender and process until smooth. Add yogurt, seasoned rice vinegar or lemon juice and salt and pepper to taste. Pulse on and off a few times just until blended. Set aside.

• On lightly greased grill over medium-high heat, cook salmon skin-side down until opaque all the way through or slightly translucent in the centre, about 8 to 10 minutes. Arrange on individual serving plates. Serve with sauce. **Makes 4 servings.**

PC Key West
Lime Juice

IF YOUR GRILL

DOESN'T HAVE A COVER,

PLACE A METAL

OR ALUMINUM FOIL PIE

PLATE OR SIMILAR-SIZED

BAKING DISH

OVER THICK FISH STEAKS

OR FILLETS TO HELP

THEM COOK THROUGH

WITHOUT OVERCHARRING.

THE PAN WILL

HELP KEEP IN THE HEAT

AND SPEED UP

THE COOKING TIME.

▾

Fish fillets and fish steaks shouldn't be left for longer than 30 to 45 minutes in an acid-based marinade — for example, those that contain vinegar, wine or lemon or lime juice — or the flesh may soften due to the action of the acid. Shrimp can go slightly longer, up to an hour. (We hate to be too rigid on this point; after all, it may have been a forgetful chef who created the classic Chinese dish, Drunken Shrimp!)

For lemon- and lime-based marinades, you can circumvent the problem by substituting finely chopped lemon or lime zest (the colored part of the peel) for juice. The zest provides a citrusy flavor without compromising the texture of the fish. It's a handy chef's trick!

GRILLED SHARK STEAK WITH KEY LIME MAYONNAISE

English visitors to Sicily in the 1800s likened swordfish to "good British beefsteak." Shark has a very similar meaty texture and mild flavor. What's more, it costs less.

4	shark steaks (each about 5 oz/150 g)	4
1/4 cup	PC Extra-Virgin Olive Oil	60 mL
1/4 cup	PC Key West Lime Juice	60 mL
2 tbsp	PC Lime Cilantro Seasoning or chopped fresh cilantro	30 mL
2 tbsp	PC Jalapeño Pepper Jelly	30 mL
1 tsp	PC Louisiana Hot Sauce	5 mL
Key Lime Mayonnaise:		
1/2 cup	PC The Ultimate Mayonnaise	125 mL
2 tbsp	PC Key West Lime Juice	30 mL
1 tbsp	PC Lime Cilantro Seasoning or chopped fresh cilantro	15 mL
3 tbsp	chopped fresh dill	45 mL

• Wipe fish with damp cloth and pat dry.
• Prepare marinade: In shallow glass bowl, mix together olive oil, lime juice, lime cilantro seasoning, jalapeño jelly and hot sauce.
• Add shark steaks and turn to coat well. Cover and let marinate at room temperature for 30 minutes.
• While fish is marinating, prepare Key Lime Mayonnaise: Mix together mayonnaise, lime juice, lime cilantro seasoning and dill. Chill until serving.
• On lightly greased grill over medium-high heat, cook fish until opaque all the way through or slightly translucent in the centre, about 3 to 5 minutes per side.
• Serve with Key Lime Mayonnaise.
Makes 4 servings.

PC Dry Garlic
Sparerib Sauce

MONKFISH (WHICH IS
ALSO KNOWN AS
ANGLER, GOOSEFISH AND,
IN FRANCE, LOTTE)
IS ONE OF THE UGLIEST,
MOST FEROCIOUS-
LOOKING CREATURES OF
THE DEEP. BUT
WHAT MONKFISH LACKS
IN BEAUTY, IT MORE
THAN MAKES UP FOR
IN FLAVOR AND TEXTURE.
THE FIRM WHITE
FLESH IS SO DELICATE
AND SWEET THAT THE
FISH IS OFTEN COMPARED
TO LOBSTER.

Dear Miss Manners: *After eating the shrimp at dinner the other night, my husband ate the bed of lettuce under it. My son was horrified. He told his dad that this was gauche. My son claims that only olives and other minute garnishes may be consumed; greens are meant to be decorative only, he says.*

Gentle Reader: *Where does your son get his manners? Not from his parents, evidently. And not from Miss Manners, who teaches that food that appears on a plate, with the exception of those items that turn out to be painted on the china, is intended to be eaten. Should you decide to teach your son correct table manners, Miss Manners believes you might start with the rule that one does not call one's father gauche.*

— spotted in the *Toronto Star*

GRILLED MONKFISH WITH MANGO & BLACK BEAN SALSA

In the event that monkfish is not available, substitute tuna or swordfish.

2 lb	monkfish fillets, about 3/4 inch (2 cm) thick	1 kg
	PC Roasted Garlic-Flavored Olive Oil	
	Salt and freshly ground pepper	

Mango & Black Bean Salsa:

1	ripe mango, peeled and cut in 1/2-inch (1 cm) cubes	1
1	red bell pepper, cut in 1/2-inch (1 cm) cubes	1
4	green onions, finely chopped	4
1/4 cup	PC Memories of Hong Kong Spicy Black Bean and Garlic Sauce	50 mL
2 tbsp	PC Dry Garlic Sparerib Sauce	25 mL
2 tbsp	PC Roasted Garlic-Flavored Olive Oil	25 mL
1 tsp	PC Seasoned Rice Vinegar or fresh lemon juice	5 mL
1	clove PC Fresh Peeled Garlic, finely chopped	1

• Cut fish into 1 1/2-inch (4 cm) chunks. Brush all over with olive oil. Season with salt and pepper to taste. Let marinate at room temperature while preparing salsa.

• Prepare Mango & Black Bean Salsa: Mix together mango, red pepper, green onions, Memories of Hong Kong sauce, garlic sparerib sauce, olive oil, rice vinegar or lemon juice and garlic. Season with salt and pepper to taste. Set aside.

• On lightly greased grill over medium-high heat, cook fish 3 to 4 minutes per side or until natural divisions of the flesh begin to separate and fish is opaque throughout. Arrange chunks on platter. Serve with salsa.

Makes 4 to 6 servings.

Miss Manners excerpt reprinted by permission of
United Feature Syndicate.

PC Fresh Peeled Garlic

▲

CANADA'S DEPARTMENT OF FISHERIES GAINED FAME AROUND THE WORLD FOR FORMULATING A NEARLY FOOLPROOF GUIDE TO FISH COOKING TIMES. AS A GENERAL RULE, COOK FISH 10 MINUTES PER INCH (2.5 CM) THICKNESS (MEASURED AT THICKEST POINT). SOME PEOPLE COOK FISH 1 OR 2 MINUTES LESS SINCE FISH CONTINUES TO COOK SLIGHTLY WHEN IT'S OFF THE GRILL.

▼

Many people prefer arctic char to salmon, whose flesh it resembles, because it's more delicate in flavor — yet more distinctive than, say, sole or flounder.

Arctic char is related to the trout. It's found in polar waters, although a landlocked variety has adapted to Alpine lakes, where the species appears to have headed during the Ice Ages in search of colder waters.

Like the salmon, wild arctic char swim up river to spawn. In July, the maturing male fish are a beautiful olive green and their flesh is white. (We were fortunate to come by one from an arctic char farm for this photograph.) Females dwindle in size, since they will go without eating for as long as two months when they're spawning. Ordinarily, the flesh of both the male and female arctic char has a pale rosy hue.

ARCTIC CHAR WITH OREGANO & LIME

Oregano and lime are a superb complement to the flavor of the fish. If arctic char isn't available, substitute whole salmon or rainbow trout.

2	whole arctic char (each about 2 lb/1 kg), heads left on or removed	2
	PC Roasted Garlic-Flavored Olive Oil	
1 cup	chopped fresh oregano	250 mL
4	cloves PC Fresh Peeled Garlic, finely chopped	4
1/4 cup	PC Key West Lime Juice	50 mL
	Salt and freshly ground pepper	
	Fresh herbs and lime slices for garnish	

• Wipe fish with damp cloth and pat dry.
• Cut three shallow diagonal slashes into both sides of each fish so that the marinade can penetrate the flesh.
• Rub fish all over with olive oil. Mix together oregano and chopped garlic. Pat oregano-garlic mixture all over each fish; place a generous amount in cavities.
• Place fish in shallow dish; cover and let marinate for 30 minutes.
• While grill is heating, sprinkle fish and herb mixture with lime juice. Season with salt and pepper to taste.
• Place in grill basket and cook over medium heat until fish is opaque all the way through or slightly translucent in the centre, about 5 to 7 minutes per side.
• Arrange fish on platter. Garnish with lime slices and fresh herbs.
Makes 4 to 6 servings.

PC Zipper Back
Raw Shell-On Jumbo
Black Tiger Shrimp

What soya sauce is to mild-tasting Cantonese food, fermented black beans are to spicy Szechwan and Hunan cooking, two regional Chinese cuisines that figure prominently in the culinary landscape of Hong Kong. In fact, black beans predate soya sauce as a seasoning in China.

Cantonese-style food is for many of us an introduction to soya sauce. Most Chinese take-out food is Cantonese in origin. And so is the stir-fry you make for dinner. This style of cooking was brought to Canada by the men who worked on the railroad early this century. Most of them came from the Canton region, which runs along the southeast coast of China.

We wouldn't think of leaving soya sauce out of most stir-fries any more than people in China's southwestern provinces would leave the fermented black beans out of their traditional dishes. PC Memories of Hong Kong Spicy Black Bean and Garlic Sauce brings their style of cooking right to your dinner table. It's made with fermented black beans along with an authentic addition of garlic, ginger and chilies.

FIERY THAI SHRIMP WITH BLACK BEAN & GARLIC SAUCE

The pungency of salted black beans is an excellent way to heighten the sweet-tasting flesh of shrimp. Some people gnaw on the shells to extract every last bit of flavor.

3/4 cup	PC Memories of Hong Kong Spicy Black Bean and Garlic Sauce	175 mL
3 tbsp	PC Memories of Thailand Fiery Thai Dipping Sauce or PC Memories of Bangkok Spicy Thai Sauce	45 mL
1 lb	PC Zipper Back Raw Shell-On Jumbo Black Tiger Shrimp (21-30 count), thawed	454 g

◆ Combine Memories of Hong Kong sauce with Memories of Thailand or Memories of Bangkok sauce. Add shrimp and toss to coat. Let marinate at room temperature for about 1 hour.
◆ Prior to cooking, soak wooden skewers in water for at least 30 minutes.
◆ Thread shrimp onto skewers (estimate about 4 shrimp per skewer; do not overcrowd). Place shrimp on grill over medium-high heat and cook for about 2 to 3 minutes per side or just until opaque. Do not overcook.
Makes 4 servings.

PC Memories of Kyoto
Ginger Sauce

Sometimes afterthoughts are better than memories. That's how John Maxwell explains his recipe for ginger-and-coriander shrimp made with, not one, but two President's Choice sauces.

The owner of Allen's, on the Danforth, and Orso, on John St., has been playing around with our bottled PC "Memories of . . ." sauces since the first ones were introduced in 1990. "I do tons of things with all of the sauces," says John. "Since I prepare a lot of food on cooking stones, I'll often use the sauces as bases for my marinades and dipping sauces. But I doctor them up quite a bit."

Cook's instinct is what drives the well-known Toronto restaurateur to create brand new sauces from our bottled sauces, combining this one with that, and then whisking in whatever other ingredients to round out the flavor. The tastebuds guide, the hand measures. After all, preparing food should be a matter of cooking to one's taste. That's John's message. You won't hear any argument from us.

JOHN MAXWELL'S JUMBO TIGER SHRIMP WITH GINGER & CORIANDER

"I've developed quite a few recipes using PC Memories of Kyoto," says the Toronto restaurateur. "This is one of them." We published a stove-top adaptation of John's fabulous shrimp dish in the first President's Choice cookbook. Here's how he originally prepared it — on the barbecue.

1 cup	PC Memories of Kyoto Ginger Sauce	250 mL
1/4 cup	PC Memories of Thailand Fiery Thai Dipping Sauce	50 mL
1/4 cup	PC Naturally Brewed Soya Sauce or tamari sauce	50 mL
1/2 cup	dry sherry	125 mL
2 tbsp	Worcestershire sauce	25 mL
2 tbsp	PC Chopped Garlic in Oil	25 mL
2 tbsp	PC Puréed Ginger	25 mL
1/4 cup	chopped fresh coriander	50 mL
2 lb	PC Zipper Back Raw Shell-On Jumbo Black Tiger Shrimp (21-30 count), thawed	907 g

• Mix together Memories of Kyoto sauce, Memories of Thailand sauce, soya or tamari, sherry, Worcestershire, garlic, ginger and coriander. Remove 1/2 cup (125 mL) to use as a dipping sauce and set aside.
• Add shrimp to marinade and let marinate at cool room temperature or in refrigerator for 1 to 2 hours.
• Place shrimp in grill basket and grill over medium-high heat for about 3 minutes per side or just until opaque. Do not overcook.
• Serve with reserved sauce for dipping.
Makes 4 servings.

PC Zipper Back
Raw Shell-On Colossal
Black Tiger Shrimp

Fresh coriander, also called cilantro and Chinese parsley, is an acquired taste — either you love it or hate it. If it's the latter, don't give up. Many people overcome their initial dislike and end up using it by the bunch!

SHRIMP & SCALLOP KEBABS WITH CORIANDER PESTO

When buying coriander, look for leaves with an even green color and no wilting. Store coriander in a glass of water with a plastic bag over the leaves. They may be refrigerated in this manner for a week, but change the water every two days.

2 lb	PC Zipper Back Raw Shell-On Colossal Black Tiger Shrimp (13-20 count), thawed	907 g
2 lb	large sea scallops (about 25 to 30)	1 kg
1/4 cup	PC Extra-Virgin Olive Oil	50 mL
2 tbsp	PC Chopped Garlic in Oil	30 mL
1 to 2 tbsp	fresh lemon juice	15 to 30 mL
Coriander Pesto:		
1	bunch fresh coriander	1
2 tbsp	PC Roasted Garlic-Flavored Olive Oil	25 mL
1 tbsp	PC Seasoned Rice Vinegar	15 mL
2 tsp	PC Key West Lime Juice	10 mL
2 tsp	PC Puréed Ginger	10 mL
1 tsp	PC Louisiana Hot Sauce	5 mL
	Salt	

• Prepare Coriander Pesto first: In food processor, combine coriander, olive oil, rice vinegar, lime juice, ginger and hot sauce. Process until finely blended but not completely smooth. Add a little salt to taste. Chill until serving.

• Thread shrimp alternately with scallops on skewers, using about 3 shrimp and 2 scallops per skewer. (If using wooden skewers, soak first in water for 30 minutes.)

• In shallow glass dish, combine olive oil, garlic and lemon juice. Add kebabs and turn to coat. Cover and marinate in refrigerator for 1 to 2 hours. Let return to room temperature before cooking.

• On greased grill over medium-high heat, cook kebabs for 3 to 4 minutes per side or just until scallops are nicely browned and shrimp are opaque. Do not overcook.

• Serve with Coriander Pesto.

Makes 4 to 6 servings.

CASUAL
OPTIONS

PC Italian Magic
Homestyle Italian Sauce

Nearly everyone loves traditional barbecue fare: ribs, steaks, burgers, hot dogs. But when you feel like a change, there's no better antidote to summer barbecue ennui than twirling a few forkfuls of angel hair pasta in a simple sauce made with lightly charred kernels of sweet corn, juicy grilled shrimp and President's Choice Italian Magic Homestyle Sauce.

GRILLED CORN & GARLIC SHRIMP WITH ANGEL HAIR PASTA

The combination of grilled corn and shrimp in this sensational pasta dish is nothing short of sublime. Serve with crusty bread, tossed salad greens and a bottle of dry white wine. For a variation, use half shrimp, half scallops.

1 lb	PC Zipper Back Raw Shell-On Black Tiger Shrimp, thawed (21-30 count)	454 g
4	cloves PC Fresh Peeled Garlic, finely chopped	4
3 or 4	ears of corn, shucked	3 or 4
2 tbsp	PC Extra-Virgin Olive Oil	25 mL
2	PC Fresh Shallots, finely chopped	2
2 cups	PC Italian Magic Homestyle Italian Sauce	500 mL
1	pkg (15.9 oz/450 g) PC World's Best Capelli d'Angelo (angel hair pasta)	1
	Salt and freshly ground pepper	
1/4 cup	chopped fresh parsley	50 mL

• In medium-size bowl, combine shrimp with half the garlic. Toss well.
• Place corn on lightly greased grill over medium-high heat and cook, turning periodically, until lightly browned all over, about 8 to 10 minutes.
• Place shrimp in grill basket and grill about 3 minutes per side or just until flesh is opaque.
• Using sharp knife, cut kernels off cobs of corn. Set corn and shrimp aside.
• In large saucepan, heat oil. Add shallots and remaining garlic and cook just until fragrant, about 30 seconds; do not brown.
• Stir in Italian Magic and bring to boil, stirring occasionally; reduce heat and simmer for a few minutes.
• In large pot of boiling salted water, cook pasta until tender but firm. Drain well. Place in large pasta bowl. Add tomato sauce, shrimp, corn and salt and pepper to taste.
• Sprinkle with parsley. Toss and serve.
Makes 4 servings.

PC Memories of
Hong Kong
Barbecue Sausages

Considering that pasta has been around Italy for about 600 years, it's not surprising that the country produces literally hundreds of shapes. Commercial pasta makers have in excess of 400 pasta dies to choose from, some of them intricate enough to be dipped in gold and made into charm bracelets with no one the wiser! Italians are fierce about what shape for what sauce, although there's no consensus of opinion among families or even within a single family as to what those combinations should be.

Radiatore means "little radiators." One of the fun shapes, they're used in this recipe because they hold the sauce well.

RADIATORE WITH GRILLED SAUSAGE, FENNEL & ONIONS

For a more dramatic presentation, chop the vegetables and sausages into larger chunks. By the way, quattro formaggi *means "four cheeses."*

1	fennel bulb	1
1	large red onion	1
2 tbsp	PC Extra-Virgin Olive Oil	25 mL
	Salt and freshly ground pepper	
3 or 4	PC Memories of Hong Kong Barbecue Sausages	3 or 4
1	pkg (15.9 oz/450 g) PC World's Best Radiatore	1
1½ cups	PC Splendido Quattro Formaggi Pasta Sauce or PC Italian Magic Homestyle Italian Sauce	375 mL
¼ cup	chopped fresh basil or parsley	50 mL
½ cup	freshly shaved or grated Pecorino Romano cheese	125 mL

• Trim feathery stalks off fennel and reserve for other use. Cut fennel bulb lengthwise through core into ¼-inch (5 mm) slices. (Cutting through core helps keep slices intact.)

• Slice onion in half vertically through root. Cut each half into 5 or 6 wedges, cutting through root so wedges hold together.

• Gently toss fennel and onion with oil and a little salt and pepper to taste.

• On greased grill over medium-high heat, cook fennel, onion and sausages, turning often, until fennel and onion are tender and lightly charred and sausages are well browned, about 8 to 10 minutes. Slice sausages in half lengthwise; then slice each half diagonally into ¼-inch (5 mm) slices.

• In large pot of boiling salted water, cook pasta until tender but firm; drain well. Meanwhile, in small saucepan, heat pasta sauce just until hot.

• Place pasta in large bowl. Add sauce and toss to coat. Add fennel, onion, sausage and basil. Toss gently. Serve with cheese on top.

Makes 4 servings.

RONY'S MUSHROOM RISOTTO WITH BLACKENED CHICKEN

This goes faster if you delegate the job of grilling the chicken while you prepare the risotto. Grant the task to your favorite sous chef.

PC Memories of Gilroy Creamy Roasted Garlic Sauce

▲

RONY ZIBARA, PC COOKBOOK DESIGNER AND ART DIRECTOR, INVENTED THIS FLAVOR-RICH, SATISFYING RISOTTO ONE NIGHT WHEN HE COULDN'T THINK OF ANYTHING ELSE TO MAKE! BORN AND RAISED IN BEIRUT, RONY IS PASSIONATE ABOUT HIS LEBANESE HERITAGE AND ITS INTRIGUING CUISINE. HE ALSO ADMITS TO A LOVE OF ITALIAN AND FRENCH FOOD.

▼

2 or 3	PC Frozen Chicken Breasts for the Grill, thawed	2 or 3
1/2 cup	PC Memories of Gilroy Creamy Roasted Garlic Sauce	125 mL
2 tsp	PC Creamed Horseradish	10 mL
	Salt and freshly ground pepper	
2 tbsp	PC Unsalted Normandy-Style Cultured Butter	30 mL
2 tbsp	PC Extra-Virgin Olive Oil	30 mL
3/4 cup	finely chopped onion	175 mL
2	portobello mushrooms (4 inches/10 cm in diameter), coarsely chopped	2
6 cups	(approx.) hot chicken stock, homemade or made with PC Fresh Concentrated Chicken Stock	1.5 L
1 1/2 cups	arborio rice (available in many supermarkets)	375 mL
3/4 cup	dry red wine	175 mL
1	yellow or orange bell pepper, finely chopped	1
1/3 cup	freshly grated Pecorino Romano or Sardo cheese	75 mL

• Brush chicken with Memories of Gilroy sauce and horseradish; season with salt and pepper to taste. Let marinate for 1 hour at room temperature.

• On lightly greased grill over medium-high heat, cook chicken until cooked through and nicely charred, about 6 to 8 minutes per side. Discard skin and tear or slice chicken into pieces. Set aside.

• In small skillet, heat 1 tbsp (15 mL) each of butter and oil. Add onion and cook for a few minutes until tender. Add mushrooms and cook, stirring often, for about 5 minutes. Remove from heat.

• In saucepan over medium-high heat, bring chicken stock to boil. Reduce heat and keep at simmer while preparing risotto.

• In separate saucepan, heat remaining 1 tbsp (15 mL) each butter and oil. Stir in arborio rice and cook for about 1 minute, stirring constantly. Stir in wine and continue stirring until most of wine is absorbed.

• Add chicken stock, about 3/4 cup (175 mL) at a time, stirring continuously and waiting until most of liquid is absorbed before adding next instalment.

• Continue in this manner until rice is tender but slightly resistant to the bite, about 18 minutes; with last addition of stock, add mushrooms, chicken and yellow pepper.

• Stir in cheese. Season with salt and pepper to taste.

Makes 4 to 6 servings.

PC Memories of
Fuji Shiitake
Mushroom Sauce

▲

MICROWAVE POLENTA

**MICROWAVE OVENS
ARE GREAT FOR POLENTA
BECAUSE THERE'S NO
STICKING, NO STIRRING.
SIMPLY MIX TOGETHER
POLENTA INGREDIENTS IN
MICROWAVEABLE BOWL;
COOK, UNCOVERED, ON
HIGH FOR 12 MINUTES,
STIRRING ONCE. LET
STAND 3 MINUTES
BEFORE TURNING INTO
LOAF PAN. COVER AND
CHILL UNTIL SET.**

▼

First the homeland, then polenta! That's the gastronomic battle cry that has been bringing together members of the Prima Patria Poi Polenta society (P.P.P.P.) in Italy since the early 1700s. Even France pays homage to cornmeal mush through its Académie des Polentophages, which has been active for almost two centuries.

GRILLED POLENTA WITH CARAMELIZED ONIONS & GORGONZOLA

Polenta, a blend of cornmeal and water, is characteristically bland. But when PC Memories of Fuji Shiitake Mushroom Sauce is added to the cooking liquid, it imparts a deep, rich flavor. In this recipe, the polenta is briefly grilled, then topped with a mixture of sweet caramelized onions and pungent Gorgonzola cheese. Serve as an appetizer, side dish or light meal.

3 cups	water	750 mL
1 tsp	PC Fresh Concentrated Chicken Stock	5 mL
1/2 cup	PC Memories of Fuji Shiitake Mushroom Sauce	125 mL
1/2 tsp	salt	2 mL
1 1/2 cups	cornmeal	375 mL
1/4 cup	PC Extra-Virgin Olive Oil	50 mL
2	large onions, thinly sliced	2
1/2 cup	crumbled Gorgonzola cheese	125 mL
	PC Roasted Garlic-Flavored Olive Oil	

• In saucepan over medium-high heat, bring water to boil. Stir in chicken stock until blended. Add Memories of Fuji sauce and salt.

• Gradually add cornmeal, whisking constantly. Reduce heat to medium and cook, stirring constantly, until mixture is thick, about 5 minutes.

• Spoon cornmeal mixture into buttered 9-inch (2 L) loaf pan. Cover with plastic wrap and refrigerate until chilled.

• In skillet over medium-high heat, heat extra-virgin olive oil. Add onions, reduce heat to medium and cook, stirring often, until wilted and golden, about 20 to 25 minutes. Watch carefully to avoid burning onions. Remove from heat and stir in Gorgonzola cheese.

• Cut polenta into 1/2-inch (1 cm) slices, or, if desired, cut into creative shapes. Lightly brush all over with roasted garlic-flavored olive oil and place on grill over high heat. Cook about 3 minutes per side or until polenta becomes crisp and golden brown.

• Arrange on large platter or individual plates and top with onion and Gorgonzola mixture.

Makes 4 to 6 servings.

There's one food that has as long and as honorable a history of pit-cooking as meat, and that's beans. Native North American Indians cooked beans in clay pots in "earth ovens" lined with hot stones and the early settlers adopted this slow-cooking method for making "baked" beans.

In Italy, haricot beans — the family name for varieties such as Great Northern, navy, kidney, pinto and black beans — became popular even faster than that other New World discovery, corn. The Italians, too, learned to cook them in the fire (see sidebar).

GRILLED ENDIVE & RADICCHIO WITH TUSCAN-STYLE BEANS

A perfect light lunch or dinner — serve with crusty bread and chilled white wine.

4	heads Belgian endive	4
1	head radicchio	1
1/2 cup	PC Memories of San Francisco Golden Gate Lemon Ginger Sauce	125 mL
1 to 2 tbsp	fresh lemon juice	15 to 30 mL
1	jar (28 oz/796 mL) PC 'Too Good To Be True!' Great Northern Beans, rinsed and drained	1
2	cloves PC Fresh Peeled Garlic, finely chopped	2
2 to 3 tbsp	chopped fresh sage	30 to 45 mL
3/4 cup	chicken stock, homemade or made with PC Fresh Concentrated Chicken Stock	175 mL
	Salt and freshly ground pepper	
	PC Unsalted Normandy-Style Cultured Butter, melted, or PC Extra-Virgin Olive Oil	

- Cut Belgian endive and radicchio through the core into quarters.
- In large bowl, mix together Memories of San Francisco sauce and lemon juice. Add endive and radicchio and toss to coat; let marinade seep in between leaves. Set aside.
- In medium-size saucepan, combine beans with garlic and sage. Add chicken stock and simmer for 5 minutes. Season with salt and pepper to taste. Turn off heat.
- Place endive and radicchio in grill basket or on greased grill over medium-high heat and cook, turning periodically, for about 8 to 10 minutes or until nicely charred.
- Arrange beans and grilled vegetables on large platter. Drizzle endive and radicchio with a little melted butter or olive oil; season with salt and pepper to taste. If desired, garnish with a few sprigs of fresh sage.

Makes 4 to 6 servings.

PC 'Too Good To Be True!' Great Northern Beans

▲

DID YOU KNOW:

FIASCO IS THE NAME OF THE TRADITIONAL HEAVY GLASS, STRAW-COVERED FLASK ASSOCIATED WITH ITALY'S CHIANTI WINE. WHEN THE LAST DROP IS DRUNK, THE STRAW IS REMOVED AND THE EMPTY BOTTLE IS USED AS A VESSEL FOR COOKING BEANS OVER A SLOW FIRE. ITS LONG NARROW NECK HELPS KEEP IN MOST OF THE FLAVOR AND AROMA.

▼

Southern-style barbecue: Texas Brisket Sandwich (left) and Pulled Pork Sandwich with a side of 5-Minute Coleslaw. Simple food, yes, and some of the best "barbecue" fare you will ever eat. You don't even have to fire up the grill! Turn page for recipes.

PC Seasoned
Rice Vinegar

▲

5-MINUTE COLESLAW

MIX TOGETHER 1 SMALL
CABBAGE, SHREDDED,
3/4 CUP (175 mL)
PC THE ULTIMATE
MAYONNAISE, 1/4 CUP
(60 mL) PC SEASONED
RICE VINEGAR AND SALT
AND FRESHLY GROUND
PEPPER TO TASTE.
IF DESIRED, ADD A LITTLE
PC DIJON MUSTARD.
CHILL UNTIL SERVING.
MAKES ENOUGH FOR
8 TO 10 SANDWICHES.

▼

We were in Dallas, visiting the folks at Tom Thumb Supermarkets (they carry 400 PC products). They were going to take us someplace special for lunch. Great! But, hey, where do we end up? In a ramshackle building where lunch lasts all of 20 minutes — on a slow day!

That's how long it takes to wolf down a barbecued brisket sandwich at Sonny Bryan's, Dallas's famous pithouse. But if superlative brisket is what you're after, this is the place to be.

The drill is casual and fun. Stand in line, place your order (brisket sandwich or ribs), grab your food and hope there's a school desk free in the cramped "dining" quarters so you can sit while you eat — otherwise you'll be eating off the hood of your car. The experience is a pithy statement about what barbecue means in Texas: Ribs or beef brisket, cooked for hours and hours in a haze of smoke, and then eaten lickety-split.

TEXAS BRISKET SANDWICH

In Texas, if it's smoked, it's barbecued. Our oven rendition of Texas-style brisket has genuine smoky savor, and the mixture tastes even better the next day. The soft hamburger buns are traditional, although you can also serve the mixture on Padas, the soft-crusted Portuguese round buns.

1	beef brisket (3 to 4 lb/1.5 to 2 kg)	1
	Salt and freshly ground pepper	
1/2 cup	boiling water	125 mL
1 cup	PC Squeezable Hickory-Smoked Gourmet Barbecue Sauce	250 mL
1 cup	PC Tournament Barbecue Sauce	250 mL
8 to 10	soft hamburger buns or crusty buns of your choice	8 to 10
	5-Minute Coleslaw (see sidebar)	

◆ Sprinkle brisket all over with salt and pepper to taste. Place fat-side up in shallow roasting pan. Add boiling water.

◆ Cover pan with aluminum foil and cook in 350°F (180°C) oven until meat is fork-tender, about 3 to 4 hours.

◆ When brisket is finished cooking, pour off pan liquid, reserving about 1/4 cup (50 mL). Skim off excess fat; set liquid aside.

◆ Place brisket on cutting board and trim off excess fat. Cut in half lengthwise and then, using two forks, pull meat into shreds. Return meat to roasting pan; add barbecue sauces and reserved pan liquid.

◆ Place roasting pan on burner over low heat and let simmer for about 5 minutes, stirring once or twice, until heated through.

◆ Serve on buns. Top meat with 5-Minute Coleslaw.

Makes 8 to 10 servings.

Barbecue land has its tomato-free zones and the Carolinas is one of them. Seasoned white vinegar is the Carolinian's mop sauce of choice, sometimes spiked with hot pepper sauce (occasionally hot enough to start a brush fire). Simple as it sounds, there may be no better match for pork butt that's cooked low and slow then pulled into shreds and piled high on a bun.

Cookbook writer Frances Litwin turned us onto this style of barbecue. We knew we had a winner on our hands when, at our tasting, the only sounds to be heard between gleeful chomping were: "Don't change a thing." "This is so-o-o good!" "I can't stop eating it!" "The best pork I've ever tasted." And the most welcome words of all in this hurly-burly world: "So what if it takes more than two hours — it takes as long as it takes!"

PULLED PORK SANDWICH

Even though the pork butt never gets within spitting distance of a glowing ember (the genuine article cooks over a pit of smoldering hickory), the flavor is that of your classic Carolinian barbecued pork sandwich. "Pulled" means shredded.

1½ cups	PC Seasoned Rice Vinegar	375 mL
¾ cup	PC Cola	175 mL
1 tsp	dried red pepper flakes	5 mL
¼ tsp	cayenne pepper	1 mL
3 or 4	cloves PC Fresh Peeled Garlic	3 or 4
2 tbsp	salt	30 mL
1 tbsp	coarsely ground pepper	15 mL
1	pork loin, preferably butt end (3 to 4 lb/1.5 to 2 kg)	1
1 tbsp	PC Seasoned Rice vinegar	15 mL
8 to 10	soft hamburger buns or crusty buns of your choice	8 to 10
	5-Minute Coleslaw (see sidebar, opposite page)	

• In large bowl, combine 1½ cups (375 mL) vinegar, cola, red pepper flakes, cayenne pepper, garlic, salt and pepper. Add pork, cover and marinate overnight in refrigerator, turning once or twice.

• Place pork in Dutch oven (discard marinade). Add cold water to cover and bring to boil over medium-high heat; reduce heat to low and simmer, partially covered, for 1 hour.

• Transfer pork to baking dish, reserving and defatting pan liquid; roast, uncovered, in 350°F (180°C) oven until tender, about 1 to 1½ hours. Let cool.

• Place pork on cutting board. Using two forks or your fingers, pull meat into shreds. Place meat in heavy pot, add just enough of reserved pan liquid to moisten and 1 tbsp (15 mL) seasoned rice vinegar. Place over medium heat for a few minutes until heated through.

• Serve on buns. Top meat with 5-Minute Coleslaw.

Makes 8 to 10 servings.

PC Memories of Lyon
Frozen Marinated
Boneless Strip Loin
Pepper Steaks

L yon, located near the heart of France at the confluence of the Rhone and Saône Rivers, is famous for its cuisine, and in particular, its use of delectable sauces. The peppercorn sauce that inspired our PC Memories of Lyon 4-Peppercorn Sauce and our PC Memories of Lyon Frozen Marinated Boneless Strip Loin Pepper Steaks is one classic example.

LYON STEAK SANDWICH WITH STILTON & PORTOBELLO MUSHROOMS

This is no ordinary sandwich. It's a stunner! Primal fare for voracious appetites — but with a French twist. It's especially beautiful when presented open-faced.

4	medium-size portobello mushrooms, stems removed	4
1/2 cup	PC Memories of Fuji Shiitake Mushroom Sauce	125 mL
1/4 cup	PC Memories of Kobe "The 2 Minute Miracle" Tamari Garlic Marinade	50 mL
1/4 cup	(approx.) PC Extra-Virgin Olive Oil	50 mL
1 tsp	dried sage	5 mL
	Salt and freshly ground pepper	
2	PC Rustico Crusty Italian-Style White Breads (each 280 g)	2
4	PC Memories of Lyon Frozen Marinated Boneless Strip Loin Pepper Steaks, thawed	4
1/2 cup	PC Memories of Lyon 4-Peppercorn Sauce	125 mL
1/2	bunch arugula, coarse stems removed	1/2
1/4 lb	Stilton cheese, thinly sliced	125 g
4 to 6	thin slices red onion	4 to 6

◆ Wipe mushrooms clean with damp cloth. Mix together Memories of Fuji sauce, Memories of Kobe sauce, 1 tbsp (15 mL) olive oil, sage and salt and pepper to taste. Add mushrooms, toss to coat and let marinate 2 hours.

◆ Cut Rustico breads in half lengthwise. Hollow out bottom and top halves, leaving a shell about 1/4 to 1/2 inch (5 to 10 mm) thick. Brush each half with a little extra-virgin olive oil.

◆ On greased grill over medium heat, grill mushrooms for 4 to 5 minutes per side or until tender. While mushrooms are cooking, add Memories of Lyon steaks to grill and cook 2 to 3 minutes per side for medium rare or to desired doneness. Shortly before meat is done cooking, add bread to grill and cook 1 to 2 minutes until lightly toasted.

◆ Brush bread halves with Memories of Lyon sauce. Arrange arugula on bottom halves. Layer with steaks, then mushrooms, then cheese. Top with onion and remaining Rustico halves, or place Rustico tops alongside.

◆ Slice each sandwich in half and serve on platter or individual plates.

Makes 4 servings.

PC Frozen Mixed
Pepper Strips

▲

*Wish I had
time for just one more
bowl of chili.*

— the (alleged) dying
words of Kit Carson

▼

Pioneer cooks were a colorful bunch that made do with what they had. Sometimes that meant lighting the fire by pouring a little gunpowder into the muzzle of a pistol, holding it close to the kindling and firing!

Making do almost certainly meant stew. Or chili con carne—beef laced with chilies, more often than not to mask the flavor of meat that was past its prime, so to speak. Chili became common jailhouse fare for this very reason, although some jails became famous for the tastiness of their "bowl of red." Prisoners accorded cooks chili scores and were known to rebel if the chili was too vile.

GRILLED CHILI STEAK SANDWICH

For casual gatherings, you can't beat these delicious sandwiches. Make lots and serve with PC Tortilla Chips and chilled glasses of PC Premium Draft Beer.

1	PC Baron of Beef Top Sirloin Steak (1½ lb/750 g)	1
4 tbsp	PC Taco Seasoning	50 mL
1 tbsp	PC Chopped Garlic in Oil	15 mL
2 tbsp	PC Uncommonly Light Pure Olive Oil	25 mL
1	large onion, sliced	1
2 tbsp	chili powder	25 mL
1 tsp	dried red pepper flakes (or more to taste)	5 mL
2 cups	PC Frozen Mixed Pepper Strips	500 mL
1	can (28 oz/796 mL) PC Plum Tomatoes, drained and coarsely chopped	1
2	PC Rustico Crusty Italian-Style White Breads (each 280 g)	2
	Salt and freshly ground pepper	
1 cup	shredded Cheddar cheese	250 mL

• Rub steak with 2 tbsp (25 mL) taco seasoning and garlic; cover and marinate in refrigerator for 2 to 4 hours.

• Meanwhile, in skillet, heat olive oil. Add onion, chili powder, dried red pepper flakes and remaining 2 tbsp (25 mL) taco seasoning. Cook, stirring, until onion is tender. Stir in mixed pepper strips and tomatoes and continue cooking, stirring often, for about 15 minutes or until mixture is quite thick.

• On lightly greased grill over medium-high heat, cook steak for 3 to 4 minutes per side or to desired doneness. Slice breads in half lengthwise and hollow out each half, leaving a shell of about ¼- to ½-inch (5 to 10 mm) thickness. Place bread on grill and toast lightly. Cut steak into ½-inch (1 cm) cubes and add to chili mixture in skillet. Add salt and pepper to taste.

• Cover Rustico bottoms with shredded Cheddar and return to grill for 1 to 2 minutes until cheese is melted. Spoon steak mixture on top. Cover with top halves of bread. Cut each sandwich in half on the diagonal and serve.

Makes 4 servings.

TAKE MEAT, FISH AND POULTRY OUT OF THE REFRIGERATOR ABOUT **20** TO **30** MINUTES BEFORE COOKING SO IT CAN "WARM" TO ROOM TEMPERATURE BEFORE PLACING IT ON THE GRILL. BE SURE NOT TO LEAVE FOOD OUT ANY LONGER THAN NECESSARY — ESPECIALLY ON HOT SUMMER DAYS.

▼

CURRIED CHICKEN SANDWICH

Some of the marinade becomes the sauce for this delectable sandwich. You can turn down the heat by cutting back on the Memories of Jaipur sauce.

1/2 cup	PC 'Too Good To Be True!' Fat-Free Plain Yogurt	125 mL
1/2 cup	PC Memories of Jaipur Curry & Passion Fruit Sauce	125 mL
2 tbsp	PC Mint Sauce	25 mL
2 tsp	PC Chopped Garlic in Oil	10 mL
4	PC Frozen Boneless Skinless Seasoned Chicken Breasts, thawed	4
2	PC Rustico Crusty Italian-Style White Breads (280 g each), halved lengthwise	2
1 cup	shredded lettuce	250 mL
2	tomatoes, thinly sliced	2
4 to 6	thin slices of red onion	4 to 6

• Prepare marinade. Mix together yogurt, Memories of Jaipur sauce, mint sauce and garlic. Reserve ¹/₂ cup (125 mL) of marinade for later use.

• In shallow glass dish, combine chicken with marinade and toss to coat. Cover and refrigerate for 6 to 8 hours or overnight, turning occasionally.

• Hollow out Rustico halves, leaving a shell of ¹/₄- to ¹/₂- inch (5 to 10 mm) thickness.

• On lightly greased grill over medium-high heat, cook chicken for 6 to 8 minutes per side or until cooked through, basting with any leftover marinade in glass dish. Shortly before chicken is done cooking, heat Rustico halves on grill until edges are lightly charred. Cut each Rustico half in two; you should have 4 bottom and 4 top portions.

• Brush all Rustico pieces with some of reserved marinade. Layer each of 4 bottom portions with lettuce, chicken, tomato and onion slices. Cover with remaining Rustico pieces and serve.

Makes 4 servings.

PC Memories of Jaipur
Curry &
Passion Fruit Sauce

▴

To get a thin crisp shell of a crust, we like to hollow out the Rustico bread (save the trimmings for bread crumbs) — but for heartier appetites, leave the bread intact.

▾

Tomato, Arugula & Asiago on Grilled Rustico

Be sure to give the arugula a good rinsing to loosen the sandy grit that clings to its leaves.

1	red bell pepper	1
2	PC Rustico Crusty Italian-Style White Breads (280 g each), halved lengthwise	2
1 tsp	PC Roasted Garlic-Flavored Olive Oil	5 mL
2	cloves PC Fresh Peeled Garlic, finely chopped	2
2 tbsp	chopped fresh rosemary	25 mL
2	ripe tomatoes, sliced	2
2	bunches fresh arugula, stems removed	2
8	slices red onion	8
1/4 cup	PC The Decadent Raspberry Balsamic Vinaigrette	50 mL
	Salt and freshly ground pepper	
8	slices Asiago cheese	8

PC Rustico Crusty
Italian-Style
White Bread

▲

ALTHOUGH ARUGULA IS A
RELATIVE NEWCOMER
TO THE NORTH AMERICAN
PRODUCE SCENE, THE
PEPPERY, NUTTY-FLAVORED
GREEN HAS BEEN
AROUND SINCE ANCIENT
ROMAN TIMES. IT ADDS A
PLEASANTLY BITTER
COUNTERPOINT TO MIXED
GREENS AND IS
DELICIOUS SAUTÉED IN
A LITTLE OLIVE OIL AND
TOSSED WITH PASTA.

▼

◆ On lightly greased grill over high heat, roast pepper until well charred all over, about 7 to 10 minutes. Place in plastic bag, seal well and let cool. Peel and slice into thin strips. Set aside.

◆ Hollow out bread halves, leaving a shell of about ¹/₄- to ¹/₂-inch (5 to 10 mm) thickness.

◆ Mix together olive oil, garlic and rosemary and brush over cut surfaces of Rustico. On grill over medium heat, lightly toast bread. Set aside.

◆ In bowl, gently toss together tomatoes, arugula, onion, red pepper strips and raspberry balsamic vinaigrette. Season with salt and pepper to taste.

◆ To assemble: Arrange cheese over bottom half of each Rustico. Top with tomato-arugula mixture. Cover with remaining bread halves.

◆ Cut sandwiches in half and serve.

Makes 4 servings.

Three Easy Pizzas (clockwise from right): Bacon, Cheese & Tomato, Roasted Red Pepper with Oyster Mushrooms and Grilled Eggplant.

And so, while others miserably pledge themselves to the insatiable pursuit of ambition and brief power, I will be stretched out in the shade, singing.

— Fray Luis de Leon (1527-91)

The Augustinian friar, or "fray," Luis de Leon is one of Spain's most famous Renaissance poets, a beloved professor remembered not only for his lyrical prose but for his acceptance of what life tossed his way, even if that meant jail. Denounced as a heretic with a Hebrew heart for trying to "improve upon" the official Church Bible, he was confined to a dungeon from 1572 to 1576, where he began some of his most famous works. ("I do not think I should miss the opportunity of this period of leisure, in which the injustice and ill will of some have placed me," he wrote.)

Not one to be permanently rattled by life's knocks, Fray Luis returned to his classroom after five years and picked up where he left off. Demonstrating his unique ability to overcome adversity, the friar greeted his devoted students with: "As we were saying yesterday. . . ." and with that, began the next chapter of his interesting life.

The point is: Attitude is everything! Attitude makes all the difference, even when it comes to pizza. Consider the stuff that comes to your house in a cardboard box, all soggy and glued to the carton. Then think of a crisp PC Splendido Italian-style Flatbread, topped with farm-fresh vegetables and served hot off the grill. Now that's pizza with attitude. Here are four quick and easy pizzas for the grill — three savory and one sweet.

▲ BACON, CHEESE & TOMATO PIZZA

BRUSH PC ORIGINAL SPLENDIDO ITALIAN-STYLE FLATBREAD WITH PC HERB & PEPPER SPICY OLIVE OIL. GRILL TOP-DOWN FOR A FEW MINUTES UNTIL LIGHTLY BROWNED. TOP WITH TOMATO SLICES, CHOPPED GREEN ONIONS, COOKED AND CRUMBLED PC NATURALLY SMOKED BACON, SHREDDED MOZZARELLA AND PC GOURMET BLEND 100% GRATED PARMESAN CHEESE. GRILL UNTIL BOTTOM IS TOASTED. TURN OFF HEAT AND COOK WITH LID DOWN UNTIL CHEESE IS MELTED. ADD SALT AND PEPPER TO TASTE. MAKES 4 TO 6 SERVINGS. ▼

GRILLED EGGPLANT PIZZA

When eggplant is grilled, it acquires a smoky flavor that evokes tastes of all the hot-weather cuisines of the Mediterranean.

1	medium-size eggplant, cut lengthwise in ¼-inch (5 mm) slices	1
2	large portobello mushrooms, stems removed	2
	PC Roasted Garlic-Flavored Olive Oil	
1	PC Original Splendido Italian-Style Flatbread (11 in/28 cm)	1
½ cup	shredded mozzarella cheese	125 mL
½ cup	shredded fontina cheese	125 mL
	Salt and freshly ground pepper	

• Brush eggplant and mushrooms with oil. On lightly greased grill over medium heat, cook until tender and lightly charred, about 8 to 10 minutes, turning halfway through. Slice into thin strips.

- Brush Splendido lightly with oil. Place top-down on grill and cook for a few minutes until top is golden brown.
- Top Splendido with eggplant and mushrooms. Sprinkle with cheeses.
- Return to grill and cook until bottom is lightly toasted. Turn off heat and cook with cover down until cheese is melted. Add salt and pepper to taste.

Makes 4 to 6 servings.

ROASTED PEPPER PIZZA WITH OYSTER MUSHROOMS

Grilled oyster mushrooms are silken in texture except for the crisp, charred edges — absolutely delicious! They're named for their appearance: The pale taupe-colored caps are reminiscent of oyster shells.

Mark McEwan, chef/proprietor of Toronto's highly acclaimed restaurant North 44°, has passed along two tips on grilling oyster mushrooms. First, brush them sparingly with oil to minimize flare-up and prevent them from darkening as they cook. "This is critical if you wish to keep them looking attractive," he says. "If there's too much oil, the fire will flare and you'll get soot on your mushrooms." Second, cook them briefly, for a shorter time than you would cremini or portobello mushrooms. "There's very little structure to an oyster mushroom so you have to be careful with it," Mark says. "It goes limp very quickly."

PC Original Splendido Italian-Style Flatbread

4 or 5	large oyster mushrooms	4 or 5
	PC Roasted Garlic-Flavored Olive Oil	
1	PC Original Splendido Italian-Style Flatbread (11 in/28 cm)	1
1	red bell pepper, roasted, peeled and cut in strips	1
4	green onions, thinly sliced on diagonal	4
1/2 cup	freshly grated Pecorino Romano cheese	125 mL
1/2 cup	PC Gourmet Blend 100% Grated Parmesan Cheese	125 mL
	Salt and freshly ground pepper	

- Brush oyster mushrooms lightly with oil. Place on grill over medium-high heat and cook for 2 to 3 minutes per side or until tender. Tear or slice into thin strips. Set aside.
- Brush Splendido lightly with oil. Place top-down on grill and cook for a few minutes until top is golden brown.
- Top with red pepper, mushroom pieces, green onions, Pecorino Romano and Parmesan cheeses. Return to grill and cook until bottom is lightly toasted. Turn off heat and cook with cover down until cheese is melted.
- Add salt and pepper to taste.

Makes 4 to 6 servings.

DESSERT SPLENDIDO

GRILL A PC ORIGINAL SPLENDIDO ITALIAN-STYLE FLATBREAD TOP-DOWN UNTIL CRISP; BRUSH WITH MELTED BUTTER, TOP WITH DRAINED, SLICED PEACHES AND SPRINKLE LIGHTLY WITH SUGAR AND CINNAMON. RETURN TO GRILL UNTIL HEATED THROUGH.

MAKES 8 SERVINGS.

SIDE DISHES
& SALADS

PC Naturally
Smoked Bacon

*Oh, potato, oh sweet-tasting starchy tuber, humble mainstay
of the table. Let us count the ways we love thee: Baked, fried, hashed,
mashed, boiled, sautéed, puréed, steamed, grated,
in a knish, in a salad, scalloped, riced, roasted, chipped, waffled...but,
above all, grilled until your skin turns a burnished umber.*

— F. J. Litwin

Cooking is made up of details. Small details, large details . . . central details, such as which meat, fish, poultry or even vegetable dish should play the starring role; plus finicky details such as the choice of understudies — the minor ingredients or seasonings with which to embellish the flavors of the major player(s).

Grilled Sweet Potatoes with Bacon is a shining example of how a construction of culinary details results in a fabulous accompaniment.

GRILLED SWEET POTATOES WITH BACON

This is a superb side dish and simple to make. The day we ran it through our test kitchen, everyone raved. "Love it!" "It's delicious!" "Very unique flavor."

1/2 cup	PC 100% Pure Maple Syrup	125 mL
2 tbsp	PC Russian-Style Sweet Mustard	30 mL
2 tbsp	PC Brown and Spicy Mustard	30 mL
1 tsp	PC Seasoned Rice Vinegar	5 mL
8 to 10	slices PC Naturally Smoked Bacon, cooked and crumbled	8 to 10
4	sweet potatoes	4
1/4 cup	PC Roasted Garlic-Flavored Olive Oil	50 mL
	Salt and freshly ground pepper	

◆ In medium-size bowl, mix together maple syrup, Russian-style and brown and spicy mustards, and rice vinegar. Add bacon and set aside.
◆ Pierce potatoes in a few places. Microwave at High for 3 to 4 minutes or until tender on the outside but firm in the centre.
◆ Slice potatoes into rounds of 1/4-inch (5 mm) thickness. Place in bowl with garlic-flavored olive oil and salt and pepper to taste. Toss to coat.
◆ On greased grill over medium-high heat, grill potato slices, turning frequently, until crispy and lightly charred, about 3 to 4 minutes.
◆ Add potatoes to maple syrup mixture and toss.
◆ Season with salt and pepper to taste.
Makes 4 servings.

PC Peanut Oil

*When they are seated around the divine aïoli, fragrant aïoli,
deep in color as a golden thread, where, tell me where, are those men
who do not recognize that they are brothers?*

— Frédéric Mistral
(1830-1914)

From *aïl* for garlic and the Provençal *oli* for oil, the garlicky mayonnaise called aïoli (i-OH-lee) is a hallmark of regional southern French cooking. The Provençal poet Frédéric Mistral was so partial to its pungency that he founded a journal in 1891 to sing its praises. In France, aïoli is ritually served with snails, hard-cooked eggs and a mountain of fresh cooked vegetables.

GRILLED POTATOES WITH GARLIC AÏOLI

You can replace a few spoonfuls of the peanut oil with PC Extra-Virgin Olive Oil, but don't use the olive oil exclusively as its intense flavor overpowers the aïoli. Make the aïoli up to 3 hours ahead. If using small new potatoes, slice into halves or thirds.

6 to 8	new potatoes	6 to 8
1/4 cup	PC Roasted Garlic-Flavored Olive Oil	50 mL
Garlic Aïoli:		
2	egg yolks	2
2 to 4	cloves PC Fresh Peeled Garlic, chopped	2 to 4
2 tbsp	PC Seasoned Rice Vinegar	25 mL
1 1/2 cups	(approx.) PC Peanut Oil	375 mL
	Salt and freshly ground pepper	

♦ Prepare Garlic Aïoli first: In food processor or blender, combine egg yolks, garlic and vinegar. Pulse on and off a few times until blended. With motor running, gradually add oil and continue processing until thick. Add salt and pepper to taste. Chill until serving.
♦ Pierce potatoes in several places. Place in microwave; arrange 1 inch (2.5 cm) apart in circle. Microwave at High until potatoes just start to soften, about 5 to 7 minutes. Do not overcook; potatoes should be quite firm.
♦ Slice potatoes into 1/4- to 1/2-inch (5 to 10 mm) rounds. Place in bowl along with garlic-flavored olive oil and salt and pepper to taste. Toss to coat.
♦ Arrange potatoes in single layer in grill basket(s) (you may have to do this in batches). Place on grill over high heat and cook with lid down, turning every 2 minutes, until potatoes are crisp and golden brown, about 10 to 12 minutes in total. If cooking potatoes in batches, wrap grilled potatoes loosely in foil (do not seal) and place in warm oven or at edge of grill while preparing remaining potatoes. Serve with Garlic Aïoli.
Makes 4 to 6 servings.

PC The Decadent
Caesar Dressing

The first Caesar salad never saw Rome, but it was invented by an Italian. It was made in 1926 in Mexico by chef Caesar Cardini. Cardini owned a popular restaurant in Tijuana that attracted a dedicated clientele during Prohibition from Los Angeles and San Diego, California, just across the border. Cardini's salad was made with whole tender leaves of romaine, a relatively new variety at the time, introduced by immigrants from the Mediterranean region, plus a garlicky vinaigrette and Parmesan cheese. His winning combination became a hit with the Hollywood crowd. The International Society of Epicures in Paris voted it "the greatest recipe to originate in the Americas in 50 years."

GRILLED POTATO SALAD WITH CAESAR DRESSING

This take on a Caesar uses grilled potatoes instead of romaine (not a minor variation, but a delicious one!). Potatoes hold up well on the barbecue, look fantastic and the firm, sweetish flesh and lightly charred skins marry perfectly with the smokiness of the bacon and our garlicky PC The Decadent Caesar Dressing.

24	creamers or other small new potatoes, red or white or a mixture	24
2 tbsp	PC Extra-Virgin Olive Oil	25 mL
	Salt and freshly ground pepper	
8 oz	PC Naturally Smoked Bacon	250 g
2	green onions, thinly sliced	2
1/2 cup	PC The Decadent Caesar Dressing	125 mL
	Freshly shaved Parmesan cheese (preferably Parmigiano Reggiano)	

◆ Place potatoes with skins on in saucepan and cover with cold water. Bring to boil, reduce heat and simmer for 10 minutes. Drain well.
◆ Cut potatoes in half or leave whole depending on size. Place in bowl. Add olive oil and salt and pepper to taste. Toss to coat. Place in grill basket and grill over medium-high heat for 15 to 20 minutes or until lightly browned, turning occasionally.
◆ Meanwhile, in skillet, cook bacon until crisp; let drain on paper towels. Tear into pieces.
◆ Place potatoes in medium-size serving bowl. Add bacon, green onions and Caesar dressing. Toss to coat. Season with salt and pepper to taste.
◆ Serve warm or at room temperature garnished with freshly shaved Parmesan cheese.
Makes 4 servings.

PC Pecan Creek Snack Mix

One of the greatest luxuries is to be able to command plenty of good vegetables, well served up . . . excellent potatoes, smoking hot and accompanied by melted butter of the first quality, would alone stamp merit on any dinner.

— Thomas Walker
The Art of Dining
1835

R uss Rudd, our vice-president of design services (Russ art-directed the photos for this cookbook; over the years, he and his staff have won numerous awards for their PC package designs) tried this recipe at the cottage and told us he loved it, although he did make a few necessary changes owing to a lack of certain ingredients. When we pressed for details, he divulged that the one and only constant seemed to be the potato! It just goes to show that some recipes lend themselves to endless reinterpretation. Certainly you can do almost anything you want with this salad and it will still taste wonderful.

GRILLED RED & WHITE POTATO SALAD

If you can't find small waxy new potatoes, particularly the mini "creamers" that are about 1 inch (2.5 cm) in diameter and ideal for potato salad, use slightly larger ones and cut them in halves or quarters.

1 lb	small red new potatoes	500 g
1 lb	small white new potatoes	500 g
3 tbsp	PC Extra-Virgin Olive Oil	45 mL
	Salt and freshly ground pepper	
8 oz	PC Naturally Smoked Bacon, cut in large pieces	250 g
2 cups	fresh tender green beans	500 mL
1 cup	PC Pecan Creek Snack Mix or whole fresh pecans	250 mL
1	red bell pepper, cut in julienne strips	1
1/4 cup	thinly sliced shallots	50 mL
1/2 cup	chopped green onions	125 mL
1 1/2 cups	PC The Decadent Creamy French-Style Parmesan Dressing or PC The Decadent Ranch Dressing	375 mL
2 to 3 tbsp	chopped fresh parsley	30 to 45 mL

• Cook red and white potatoes with skins on in boiling salted water to cover for about 10 to 12 minutes or until tender; do not overcook. Drain. Cut larger potatoes into halves or quarters, if desired.

• Toss potatoes with olive oil and salt and pepper to taste. Place in grill basket over medium-high heat and grill for 3 to 5 minutes, turning periodically, until potatoes are lightly charred.

• In small skillet, cook bacon until brown and crispy. Drain on paper towels. Cook green beans in boiling water to cover for 2 to 3 minutes or until tender-crisp. Drain.

• Place potatoes in serving bowl. Add bacon, pecan snack mix, red pepper, shallots, green onions and green beans. Toss. Add creamy Parmesan dressing and toss again. Sprinkle with parsley and serve.

Makes 4 to 6 servings.

**PC Rustico
Crusty Italian-Style
White Bread**

**TO BOOST THE
SMOKY FLAVOR OF FOODS
THAT REQUIRE
ONLY A SHORT GRILLING
TIME, SUCH AS BREAD,
KEEP THE LID OF
THE BARBECUE CLOSED.**

**IN ITALY, BREAD SALAD IS
CALLED *PANZANELLA*,
WHEREAS IN MOROCCO,
IT GOES BY THE NAME
*SHALADA DEL KHOBZ
YABESS*, AND IN
LEBANON, *FATTOUSH*.**

I n a salad, large chunks of dried or toasted bread not only add texture, but also mingle with the delicious juices of other ingredients — such as grilled tomatoes, roasted red peppers and fragrant extra-virgin olive oil in this superb recipe.

GRILLED BREAD SALAD WITH ROASTED PEPPERS & CHERRY TOMATOES

Bread salad is traditionally made with day-old bread, but in this version, we use grilled chunks of our popular PC Rustico Crusty Italian-Style White Bread. Grilling crisps the bread and gives the salad an outdoorsy flavor. Everyone on our tasting panel declared this salad a sensation.

1	PC Rustico Crusty Italian-Style White Bread (280 g)	1
¼ cup	(approx.) PC Extra-Virgin Olive Oil	50 mL
3	red bell peppers, cut in strips about 1 inch (2.5 cm) wide	3
2 cups	cherry tomatoes, halved	500 mL
½ cup	PC 100% Pure Maple Syrup	125 mL
2 tsp	fresh lemon juice	10 mL
1 tsp	dried oregano	5 mL
2	bunches arugula, coarse stems removed	2
1	Belgian endive, leaves separated	1

• Several hours ahead, slice bread in half lengthwise. Then slice each half lengthwise into 3 or 4 long "fingers." Let bread stand uncovered for several hours to dry out.

• Brush bread all over with some of the oil and place on grill over medium-high heat, turning often, until lightly browned all over. Then cut each "finger" into 4 elongated "cubes." Set aside.

• In medium-size bowl, combine red peppers and cherry tomatoes. Add maple syrup and toss. Add 2 tbsp (25 mL) olive oil, lemon juice and oregano and toss again. Let vegetables marinate for 20 to 30 minutes.

• Place peppers and tomatoes in grill basket, reserving marinade. Place on grill over medium-high heat and cook about 8 to 12 minutes or until lightly charred, turning carefully every few minutes.

• In bowl, combine grilled vegetables, bread cubes and reserved marinade. Toss lightly.

• Line 4 individual salad plates or one large platter with arugula and endive leaves. Arrange grilled bread, peppers and tomatoes on top.

Makes 4 servings.

O ur taste for salads, relishes and pickles at mealtime owes a lot to cooks of Dutch and German lineage. "Sweet and sour" or "sweet and salty" are long-standing traditions in the kitchens of northern Europe because the ground stayed frozen for so many months of the year; pickling allowed people to preserve the harvest. Many of our now-favorite accompaniments, such as spicy mustard, sweet pickled vegetables and *koolsla*, or "cool cabbage" salad, arose from need.

Our Fiery Corn Slaw is a cross between a Tex-Mex salsa and a Dixie-style coleslaw. It's made with corn and cabbage, but contains no mayonnaise. Instead, it's dressed with a tangy vinaigrette sweetened with maple syrup and "heated" with a little PC Memories of Thailand Fiery Thai Dipping Sauce.

PC Frozen Peaches & Cream Corn

FIERY CORN SLAW

Shredded cabbage makes a prettier slaw, but chopped cabbage is easier to spoon onto hamburgers and hotdogs. Either way, this is a great-tasting, spicy side salad. If you prefer less heat, cut back on the PC Memories of Thailand sauce.

1½ cups	PC Frozen Peaches & Cream Corn or fresh corn kernels	375 mL
½ cup	finely chopped onion	125 mL
1	red bell pepper, thinly sliced or chopped	1
½ cup	PC 100% Pure Maple Syrup	125 mL
1 cup	cider vinegar	250 mL
1 tbsp	PC Dijon Mustard	15 mL
1 tbsp	salt	15 mL
1½ tsp	dry mustard	7 mL
3 to 4 tbsp	PC Memories of Thailand Fiery Thai Dipping Sauce (or to taste)	45 to 60 mL
1	medium-size green cabbage, shredded or chopped	1

◆ In saucepan, combine corn, onion, red pepper, maple syrup, cider vinegar, Dijon mustard, salt, dry mustard and Memories of Thailand sauce. Bring to boil, reduce heat and simmer for 1 to 2 minutes. Let cool.

◆ Combine corn mixture with shredded cabbage and mix well. Refrigerate 1 to 2 hours or longer. Drain excess liquid before serving.

Makes 4 to 6 servings.

▲

SLAWS CAN BE MADE OUT OF ALMOST ANY KIND OF VEGETABLE THAT HAS BEEN CHOPPED OR FINELY SHREDDED INTO JULIENNE STRANDS — ESPECIALLY ROOT VEGETABLES SUCH AS CARROTS AND CELERIAC.

▼

PC Frozen Petits
Pois Small Sweet Peas

To be thin-skinned is a good thing — for a pea. To be small and sweet like a petit pois is even better. This special hybrid pea is small by nature, and tender, with a pleasantly sweet flavor. Yet the pea was not always so. Until the Italians developed the tiny *piselli novelli*, which so captivated members of the French court in the 1690s — it could even be eaten fresh from the pod! — peas were coarser and mostly dried and boiled for a porridge or a soup.

Good-eating peas are now so commonplace that one can easily overlook the fact that even though there is only one edible species, there are actually hundreds of different varieties, many of them shouldering names full of promise such as Little Marvel, Sugar Bon and Honey Pod.

Sweet Pea Salad

When it comes to peas, the smaller the better. Our PC Petits Pois Small Sweet Peas are filled with natural sweetness. Serve this colorful, flavor-rich salad with grilled meats and poultry — or on its own as a light lunch.

1/2	bag (2.2 lb/1 kg) PC Frozen Petits Pois Small Sweet Peas, thawed (about 2 1/2 cups /625 mL)	1/2
1/2	red bell pepper, finely chopped	1/2
1	bunch watercress (coarse stems removed), finely chopped	1
2	green onions, chopped or sliced	2
3	hard-cooked eggs, chopped	3

Dressing:

¹/₄ cup	PC Extra-Virgin Olive Oil	50 mL
2 tbsp	PC Seasoned Rice Vinegar	25 mL
1 tbsp	PC Old-Fashioned Dijon Mustard	15 mL
1 tbsp	PC Premium Alfalfa Honey	15 mL
	Salt and freshly ground pepper	

♦ In medium-size bowl, combine peas, red pepper, watercress, green onions and hard-cooked eggs.

♦ Prepare dressing: Mix together oil, vinegar, mustard, honey and salt and pepper to taste. Add dressing to salad ingredients and toss to coat. Taste and adjust seasoning.

Makes 4 to 6 servings.

Our three
terrific
salads start
with beans,
couscous
and rice.
Turn page
for recipes.

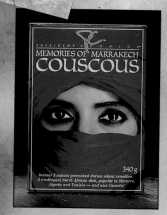

**PC Memories of
Marrakech Couscous**

COUSCOUS SALAD

Couscous replaces bulgur (cracked wheat berries) in this variation of tabbouleh.

1/2	seedless cucumber, chopped	1/2
1 tbsp	PC Chopped Garlic in Oil	15 mL
6 tbsp	PC Seasoned Rice Vinegar	75 mL
	Salt and freshly ground pepper	
1 tsp	PC Fresh Concentrated Chicken Stock	5 mL
1 1/4 cups	boiling water	300 mL
1 cup	PC Memories of Marrakech Couscous	250 mL
2	plum tomatoes, chopped	2
3 tbsp	chopped fresh mint	45 mL
1/2 cup	chopped fresh parsley	125 mL
1/4 cup	chopped red onion	50 mL
1/4 cup	PC Extra-Virgin Olive Oil	50 mL

◆ In small bowl, mix together cucumber, garlic, 1/4 cup (50 mL) rice vinegar and salt and pepper to taste. Let sit for 30 minutes.

◆ In separate bowl, mix together concentrated chicken stock and boiling water. Stir in couscous; let rest 5 minutes. Refrigerate until chilled.

◆ To couscous, add cucumber mixture, tomatoes, mint, parsley, onion, olive oil and remaining 2 tbsp (25 mL) vinegar. Toss well. Chill until serving.

Makes 6 to 8 servings.

7-BEAN SALAD WITH MINT & BASIL

Serve as a side dish or main course — either way, this is a delicious and satisfying salad.

1	jar (28 oz/796 mL) PC 'Too Good To Be True!' 7 Bean Mix, rinsed and drained	1
1	red bell pepper, chopped	1
1	fennel bulb, chopped	1
1 cup	chopped celery	250 mL
1/4 cup	finely chopped red onion	50 mL
2	cloves PC Fresh Peeled Garlic, finely chopped	2
4 to 5 tbsp	each chopped fresh basil and mint	60 to 75 mL
2 tbsp	PC Roasted Garlic-Flavored Olive Oil	25 mL
	Juice of 1 lemon	
1 tbsp	PC Balsamic Vinegar	15 mL
	Salt and freshly ground pepper	

◆ Combine 7 bean mix, red pepper, fennel, celery, onion, garlic, basil, mint, olive oil, lemon juice, balsamic vinegar and salt and pepper to taste.

◆ Toss well. Chill until serving.

Makes 6 to 8 servings.

Texmati Rice Salad

This dish was inspired by the popular wild rice salad that Dianne Cullen, a senior VP with SMW Advertising in Toronto, serves her friends. It's easily doubled or tripled.

1 cup	PC Royal Blend Texmati Premium Rice Mix	250 mL
1 tsp	PC Fresh Concentrated Chicken Stock	5 mL
2 tbsp	chopped fresh parsley	25 mL
	Salt and freshly ground pepper	
1/2	red bell pepper, roasted, peeled, seeded and chopped	1/2
3	green onions, sliced	3
1/3 cup	PC Roasted Garlic-Flavored Olive Oil	75 mL
1/4 cup	PC Balsamic Vinegar	50 mL
1/2 cup	roasted whole hazelnuts or slivered almonds	125 mL

◆ In medium-size saucepan, combine rice, 1½ cups (375 mL) cold water, concentrated chicken stock, parsley and 1 tsp (5 mL) salt. Bring to boil and stir once; reduce heat, cover and simmer for 15 minutes. Let cool.

◆ Combine rice with red pepper, green onions, olive oil, vinegar, nuts and salt and pepper to taste. Serve chilled or at room temperature.

Makes 4 servings.

PC Royal Blend Texmati Premium Rice Mix

▲

1 CUP (250 mL) OF BEANS PROVIDES THE PROTEIN EQUIVALENT OF 2 TO 3 OZ (60 TO 90 G) OF MEAT. PC 'TOO GOOD TO BE TRUE!' 7 BEAN MIX CONTAINS SMALL RED BEANS, NAVY BEANS, LIGHT RED KIDNEY BEANS, BLACK-EYED PEAS, GREAT NORTHERN BEANS, GREEN PEAS AND BABY LIMA BEANS.

▼

PC Memories of Sonoma
Dried Tomato Sauce

▲

To soften sun-dried tomatoes, plump in boiling water for 15 to 20 minutes. Drain and use immediately, or use to make your own sun-dried tomatoes in oil: Put the softened tomatoes in a jar and pour in PC Extra-Virgin Olive Oil to cover. Seal well and refrigerate for up to two weeks.

▼

un-dried tomatoes, also called *pumate*, aren't trendy. Just ask an Italian. Throughout Italy's southern regions, people have been drying tomatoes in the hot summer sun for hundreds of years — especially the fleshy plum variety and small cherry tomatoes called *sangiovannino*. In the U.S., sun-dried tomatoes are a much more recent phenomenon — popping up in the culinary landscape in the early '80s.

It takes about 17 pounds (7.7 kg) of fresh tomatoes to make 1 pound (500 g) of the sun-dried product, so the flavor is very concentrated — deeper and richer than fresh tomatoes and with a tang reminiscent of olives. The chewy, mahogany red ovals can be chopped into small pieces, left whole or rehydrated and flavored with olive oil and fresh herbs. Be warned: There is no substitution!

MEMORIES OF SONOMA TOMATO SALAD

Make this with the biggest, reddest, ripest beefsteak tomatoes you can find. (You can also mix in a few yellow tomatoes if you're lucky enough to find them.) Then drizzle with our superb dressing, which tastes far more complex than you'd ever guess from looking at the recipe. Serve with crusty bread on the side.

4 to 6	large ripe tomatoes, sliced	4 to 6
	Freshly shaved Parmesan cheese	
	(preferably Parmigiano Reggiano)	
Sonoma Dressing:		
1/2 cup	PC Memories of Sonoma Dried Tomato Sauce	125 mL
1/4 cup	sour cream or PC 'Too Good To Be True!' Low-Fat	50 mL
	Sour Cream Product	
1	clove PC Fresh Peeled Garlic, finely chopped	1
2 tbsp	chopped fresh basil	30 mL
	Salt and freshly ground pepper	

• Prepare Sonoma Dressing first: In small bowl, combine Memories of Sonoma sauce, sour cream, garlic, basil and salt and pepper to taste. Blend well. (You may also prepare dressing in a food processor; combine ingredients and pulse on and off a few times until blended.) Chill dressing while preparing salad.

• Arrange sliced tomatoes on large platter or individual salad plates. Top with shaved Parmesan cheese and salt and pepper to taste. Drizzle with dressing.
Makes 4 to 6 servings.

Tzatziki is a versatile, flavor-rich yogurt, garlic and cucumber dip and spread that is commonly used throughout Greece and the Middle East. It's a traditional accompaniment for shish kebab, but it's also excellent as a dip for chips or fresh vegetables. The best part is that our PC 'Too Good To Be True!' Tzatziki is made with a low-fat (2%), low-moisture yogurt — and derives only 25% of its calories from fat. In this delicious Greek salad, we use tzatziki as a salad dressing.

'TOO GOOD TO BE TRUE!' GREEK SALAD

This makes a wonderful light lunch with a loaf of crusty bread — or serve with our delicious Souvlaki with Roasted Garlic Oil (p. 110). For best flavor and appearance, make this salad close to serving time.

2	ripe tomatoes, cut in 1/2-inch (1 cm) cubes	2
1	seedless cucumber, cut in 1/2-inch (1 cm) cubes	1
1	red onion, thinly sliced	1
1	red bell pepper, cut in 1/2-inch (1 cm) squares	1
10 to 12	PC Super Colossal Pitted Black Olives, cut in half, or 20 small black Greek olives	10 to 12
1	container (250 g) PC 'Too Good To Be True!' Tzatziki Low-Fat Yogurt Dip & Spread	1
1 cup	crumbled feta cheese	250 mL
	Salt and freshly ground pepper	

♦ In large salad bowl, combine tomatoes, cucumber, onion, red pepper and olives. Add tzatziki, feta cheese and salt and pepper to taste. Toss gently.
♦ Chill for 15 to 20 minutes or just until slightly chilled.
♦ Taste and adjust seasoning.
Makes 4 servings.

PC 'Too Good To Be True!' Tzatziki Low-Fat Yogurt Dip & Spread

▲

PC 'TOO GOOD TO BE TRUE!' TZATZIKI IS A LOW-FAT, CHOLESTEROL-FREE YOGURT DIP AND SPREAD THAT CONTAINS ONLY 11 CALORIES PER TABLESPOON (15 mL).

▼

Gourmandise is an act of our judgment, in obedience to which we grant a preference to things that are agreeable over those that have not that quality.

—Jean-Anthelme Brillat-Savarin
(1755-1826)

GRILLED VEGETABLE FEAST

All vegetables were tested on a gas grill set at medium-high heat with the lid up. Cooking times are approximate and depend on the size and freshness of the produce.

New Potatoes

Pierce small whole potatoes with fork, place in bowl and cover with plastic wrap. Microwave at High for about 4 minutes. Place on lightly greased grill over medium-high heat for 10 to 12 minutes or until tender and lightly charred. Toss with PC Normandy-Style Cultured Butter, chopped fresh herbs (thyme, dill, tarragon, summer savory) and salt and coarsely ground pepper to taste. Or drizzle with PC Memories of Sonoma Dried Tomato Sauce.

Leeks

Trim leeks and cut in half lengthwise. Rinse well under cold water to remove grit. Arrange on plate, cover with plastic wrap and microwave at High for about 2 minutes. Place on lightly greased grill over medium-high heat for 8 to 10 minutes or until tender and lightly charred. Brush lightly with PC Memories of Asiago Tangy Asiago Cheese Sauce.

Corn

Soak in cold water with husks and silk intact for about 1 hour. Then place on grill over medium-high heat and cook for 20 to 25 minutes or until tender, turning three or four times. (Takes a while but worth the wait.) Serve with PC Normandy-Style Cultured Butter and salt and pepper to taste.

Green Onions

Trim off tops, then place on lightly greased grill over medium-high heat and cook for 10 to 15 minutes until tender. Brush with PC Memories of San Francisco Golden Gate Lemon Ginger Sauce.

Broccoli

Remove stalks. Cut whole florets in half lengthwise. Arrange in bowl and cover with plastic wrap. Microwave at High for 2 minutes. Then place on lightly greased grill over medium-high heat and cook for 10 to 12 minutes or until tender and nicely charred. Drizzle with PC Memories of Szechwan Peanut Sauce.

Sweet Potatoes

Pierce whole unpeeled potatoes in a few places with a fork. Arrange on plate and cover with plastic wrap. Microwave at High for 4 minutes. Slice into rounds just shy of 1/2-inch (1.2 cm) thickness and brush with PC Roasted Garlic-Flavored Olive Oil. Grill over medium-high heat for 10 to 12 minutes or until tender and lightly charred. Brush with equal parts PC 100% Pure Maple Syrup and PC Dijon Mustard.

Zucchini

Cut lengthwise into quarters. If zucchini is long, cut quarters into 3-inch (7.5 cm) lengths. Place on lightly greased grill over medium-high heat and cook for 15 minutes until tender and lightly charred. Serve with PC Memories of Bangkok Spicy Thai Sauce or Memories of Szechwan Peanut Sauce.

Eggplant

Leave peel on. Slice into rounds about 1/4 to 1/2 inch (5 to 10 mm) thick. Place on grill over medium-high heat and cook, turning a few times, for 10 to 15 minutes or until tender and lightly charred. Brush with PC Roasted Garlic-Flavored Olive Oil and sprinkle with salt and freshly ground pepper to taste. Serve on their own or with PC 'Too Good To Be True!' Tzatziki Low-Fat Yogurt Dip & Spread.

Mushrooms

Brush mushrooms clean or wipe with a damp cloth. Brush with PC Roasted Garlic-Flavored Olive Oil and place on lightly greased grill over medium-high heat for about 10 to 12 minutes or until tender and lightly charred, turning periodically. Cut into halves or quarters (depending on size) and toss with PC Memories of Gilroy Creamy Roasted Garlic Sauce.

Fennel

Trim off feathery tops and root end, then separate into "leaves." Cut centre in half lengthwise and discard woody core. Place on lightly greased grill over medium-high heat and cook for 10 to 15 minutes or until tender but firm and lightly charred all over. Brush with PC Roasted Garlic-Flavored Olive Oil and season with salt and pepper to taste. Serve with freshly shaved Parmigiano Reggiano cheese.

Red or Vidalia Onions

Slice crosswise into rounds about 1/4 inch (5 mm) thick or cut in half through core and cut each half into 4 to 6 wedges. Grill over medium-high heat until tender and lightly charred, about 10 to 12 minutes, turning a few times along the way. Brush lightly with PC Roasted Garlic-Flavored Olive Oil and drizzle with PC Balsamic Vinegar. Sprinkle with salt and coarsely ground pepper to taste.

Garlic and Shallots

Separate garlic into cloves; leave skin on. Leave skin on shallots as well; if large, separate into cloves. Toss garlic and shallots with a little PC Roasted Garlic-Flavored Olive Oil. Season with salt and pepper to taste. Thread alternately on wooden skewers that have been soaked in water for 30 minutes, then place on grill over medium-high heat and cook, turning periodically, for 30 minutes or until tender and lightly charred.

Asparagus

Break or cut tough ends off spears. Arrange asparagus on plate and cover with plastic wrap. Microwave at High for 1 minute. Place directly on grill or in grill basket over medium-high heat and cook for 8 to 10 minutes or until tender and lightly charred, turning periodically. Serve with PC Memories of San Francisco Golden Gate Lemon Ginger Sauce.

Carrots

Slice carrots in half lengthwise, then cut each half into 3-inch (7.5 cm) lengths. Arrange on plate, cover with plastic wrap and microwave at High for 2 to 4 minutes, depending on thickness and firmness. Place carrots on grill over medium-high heat and cook for 15 to 20 minutes, turning occasionally, until tender but firm and lightly charred. Serve with PC Memories of San Francisco Golden Gate Lemon Ginger Sauce.

Radicchio

Cut radicchio into quarters; brush with PC Extra-Virgin Olive Oil or PC Roasted Garlic-Flavored Olive Oil. Place on grill over medium-high heat and cook for 10 to 12 minutes, turning periodically, until nicely charred. Squeeze fresh lemon juice all over. Season with salt and coarsely ground pepper to taste.

Bell Peppers

Leave peppers whole or cut in half and remove seeds and ribs. Place on lightly greased grill over medium-high heat and cook for 20 to 25 minutes or until tender and nicely charred. Slice and brush with PC Roasted Garlic-Flavored Olive Oil; sprinkle with chopped fresh basil. Peppers may be peeled, if desired: Remove from grill and place in plastic bag; seal well and let cool. Peel and use immediately or cover and store in refrigerator for up to 3 days.

DESSERTS & REFRESHERS

PC Memories of
Ancient Damascus
Tangy Pomegranate
Sauce

▲

THE RUBY RED JUICE OF

THE POMEGRANATE

ENHANCES BOTH SAVORY

AND SWEET DISHES.

BOILED-DOWN

POMEGRANATE JUICE OR

"POMEGRANATE

MOLASSES" IS A STAPLE

IN MIDDLE EASTERN

COOKING. EVEN THE

ITALIANS HAVE BEEN

KNOWN TO USE

POMEGRANATE JUICE AT

THEIR BARBECUES

TO BASTE SPIT-ROASTED

TURKEY.

▼

A popular fruit dessert consists of strawberries tossed gently with a bit of sugar and balsamic vinegar. (The vinegar brings out the natural sweetness of the berries.) That idea was the impetus for this attractive dessert in which PC Memories of Ancient Damascus Tangy Pomegranate Sauce becomes the glaze for a dessert kebab made with strawberries and pineapple. Unusual and also delicious!

PINEAPPLE & STRAWBERRY BROCHETTES

PC Memories of Ancient Damascus Tangy Pomegranate Sauce complements the natural sweetness of pineapple and strawberries in this easy-to-make dessert.

1	pineapple, peeled, cored and cut in 1-inch (2.5 cm) cubes (about 6 cups/1.5 L)	1
4 cups	large firm strawberries, hulled	1 L
1 cup	PC Memories of Ancient Damascus Tangy Pomegranate Sauce	250 mL
1	tub (2 L) PC The Decadent Chocolate Fudge Crackle Ice Cream	1

♦ Soak wooden skewers in water for 30 minutes before using.
♦ Place pineapple cubes and strawberries in large bowl. Add Memories of Ancient Damascus sauce and toss gently to coat. Let fruit marinate for about 20 to 30 minutes.
♦ Thread pineapple onto skewers, using about 4 or 5 cubes per skewer. Then thread strawberries onto remaining skewers, using about 4 or 5 berries per skewer, depending on size. (Do not alternate pineapple and berries on the same skewer because they require very different grilling times.)
♦ Place pineapple on grill over medium-high heat and cook 6 to 8 minutes, turning and basting often with leftover Memories of Ancient Damascus sauce, until heated through and lightly caramelized. About 2 to 3 minutes before pineapple is done, add skewers of strawberries to grill and cook just until heated through; do not overcook or berries will get mushy.
♦ Scoop chocolate crackle ice cream onto individual dessert plates. Arrange one or two skewers of pineapple and one of strawberries on each plate.
Makes about 6 servings.

Eat the pomegranate, for it purges the system of envy and hatred.

— The Prophet Mohammed
(570-632)

PC Vanilla Crème
Anglaise

In its simplest terms, clafoutis (kla-foo-TEE) is fruit baked in a pancake batter. Some liken it to a fruit-filled Yorkshire pudding (it does puff up as it cooks!). Cherries have traditionally occupied centre stage, but over the years, other fruits have crept in as more people have discovered the delights of this home-style dessert and begun experimenting with their favorites. Apricots, plums, prunes and figs are all candidates for a clafoutis. Our version is made with mixed fresh berries and PC Vanilla Crème Anglaise — a snap to make.

MIXED BERRY CLAFOUTIS

This sumptuous dessert looks and tastes richer than it actually is. PC Vanilla Crème Anglaise gives the "batter" the mouth feel of a luxurious custard, but with significantly less butterfat — only about 17% compared with 35% in whipping cream. Mix and match the berries according to your taste preferences or budget. (We liked using 1 pint of blueberries with ½ pint each of raspberries and blackberries.)

1	container (500 mL) PC Vanilla Crème Anglaise	1
3	eggs	3
3 tbsp	granulated sugar	45 mL
2 tbsp	all-purpose flour	25 mL
1 tsp	grated lemon zest	5 mL
5 cups	mixed fresh berries: Blueberries, raspberries and/or blackberries	1.2 L
	Icing sugar	
	Additional PC Vanilla Crème Anglaise (optional)	

♦ In medium-size bowl, mix together vanilla crème anglaise, eggs, sugar, flour and lemon zest until blended. Pour ⅓ of mixture into buttered 10-inch (25 cm) pie plate.

♦ Bake in 400°F (200°C) oven for 7 minutes or until custard just starts to set around edges.(This prevents fruit from sinking to bottom.)

♦ Add fruit and remaining crème anglaise mixture. Continue baking 40 to 45 minutes or until custard is set and top is golden brown. Let cool 15 to 20 minutes.

♦ Sift a little icing sugar over top, then slice and serve. If desired, drizzle a little crème anglaise over each portion.

Makes 6 to 8 servings.

PC Extra Thick Sliced
Cinnamon Bread
with Raisins

*To avoid temptation,
yield.*

— old range saying

O n the way to the airport to catch a flight back from the Memphis world barbecue competition (see Memphis Memoirs, p. 100), we stopped for lunch at Café Roux. This Louisiana-style eatery devotes itself to Cajun and Creole specialties, such as simmered greens and jambalayas, spicy sausages and "voodoo chicken." After going through all 14 pages of the menu, pausing briefly to consider the bisques and gumbos and "coo-nas" crusts — pizzas with Louisiana heat — Russ Rudd, our vice-president of design services and the man responsible for art-directing the photos in this cookbook, closed the menu and ordered the caramel bread pudding. Bingo! It was rich and cinnamony and served warm on a pool of swirled caramel and custard sauces.

MEMORIES OF CAFÉ ROUX BREAD PUDDING WITH VANILLA CRÈME ANGLAISE

This sensational dessert recreates what we loved best about Café Roux's special bread pudding. Using PC products keeps it simple and makes it fast. Add it to your repertoire of dessert ploys for extending the pleasure of good company.

12	slices PC Extra Thick Sliced Cinnamon Bread with Raisins	12
6 tbsp	PC Unsalted Fresh-Churned Butter, softened	90 mL
1/4 cup	PC Gourmet Butterscotch Ice Cream and Dessert Topping	60 mL
1	container (500 mL) PC Vanilla Crème Anglaise	1
1	egg	1
1/4 tsp	salt	1 mL
	Additional PC Vanilla Crème Anglaise for topping (optional)	

◆ Trim crust off bread and spread one side of each slice with butter. Arrange 6 bread slices buttered-side up in single layer in 11 x 7-inch (2 L) buttered baking dish. Drizzle all over with half of butterscotch topping.
◆ Repeat with remaining bread and butterscotch topping.
◆ Mix together crème anglaise, egg and salt. Pour evenly over bread.
◆ Bake in 350°F (180°C) oven for 40 minutes or until custard is set and top is golden brown.
◆ Serve warm with additional crème anglaise, if desired.
Makes 6 to 8 servings.

PC 'Too Good To Be True!' Just Peanuts Old-Fashioned Creamy Peanut Butter

▲

FROZEN PEANUT
BUTTER CUPS
───────

COMBINE CREAM CHEESE,
PEANUT BUTTER, ICING
SUGAR AND WHIPPED
CREAM AS PER PIE
RECIPE. SPOON INTO
PAPER-LINED MUFFIN
CUPS AND FREEZE UNTIL
FIRM. LET SOFTEN
SLIGHTLY BEFORE
SERVING. DRIZZLE WITH
PC GOURMET CHOCOLATE
ICE CREAM AND DESSERT
TOPPING AND/OR
SPRINKLE WITH CHOPPED
PEANUTS. MAKES 6 TO 8
SERVINGS.

▼

Psychologists say children like to eat the same thing every day because there's a security in sameness. That must be why we grown-ups are so comforted by the familiar flavors of our youth. (It's the child in us.)

Take peanut butter, for example. The ground-up goober reaches its zenith in Peanut Butter Pie. Cookbook writer Frances Litwin has a special weakness for this flavor-packed dessert. Our version of her long-time family favorite has a rich chocolate topping.

PEANUT BUTTER PIE

This pie, with or without its chocolate topping, is rich. It's lighter than cheesecake in texture, but keep portions small — you can always come back for seconds.

15	PC Peanut Butter First Cookies	15
1/4 cup	PC Unsalted Normandy-Style Cultured Butter, softened	60 mL
1	pkg (250 g) PC Memories of Winnipeg Old-Fashioned Cream Cheese, softened	1
1 cup	PC 'Too Good To Be True!' Just Peanuts Old-Fashioned Creamy Peanut Butter	250 mL
2 cups	icing sugar	500 mL
1 1/2 cups	whipping cream, whipped	375 mL
1/4 cup	chopped PC Dry Roasted Peanuts, lightly seasoned or unsalted	60 mL
1/2	bar (17.6 oz/500 g) PC Bittersweet Rich Dark Chocolate	1/2
1/2 cup	PC Vanilla Crème Anglaise	125 mL

• In food processor or blender, process cookies to a fine crumb. Add butter and pulse on and off a few times just until blended. Press along bottom and partly up sides of 9-inch (23 cm) deep-dish pie plate or springform pan.
• Cream together cream cheese and peanut butter until light and fluffy. Gradually blend in icing sugar, 1/2 cup (125 mL) at a time, beating well after each addition. Fold in whipped cream.
• Spoon peanut butter mixture into crumb crust. Refrigerate for 3 to 4 hours until firm.
• Prepare chocolate icing: In top of double boiler over hot (not boiling) water, melt chocolate until smooth. Let cool slightly. Stir in crème anglaise.
• Pour chocolate mixture over top of pie. Sprinkle with chopped nuts.
• Refrigerate about 30 minutes until set.

Makes 6 to 8 servings.

The French have a synonym for sweets: *entremets*. In the old days, however, the term entremets (literally "between dishes") signified any dish — be it sweet, savory or salted — that came after the spit-roasted meat or the fish course.

Entremets provided a change of pace in feasts that tended to be top-heavy with meats. They could also be greatly entertaining in that they weren't always confined to food. One of the most theatrical entremets on record, according to *Larousse Gastronomique*, was "a gigantic pâté . . . followed by a circus show with trumpet players and an elephant, and a procession of knights and ladies . . . ."

If you want to delight and even shock your guests, try a fancy Frozen Rainbow Pâté. With its layering of four flavors — passion fruit, key lime, raspberry and mango — it provides its own fanfare. The shock comes when you tell your guests you made it simply by layering four President's Choice sherbets in a loaf pan.

PC Key Lime Sherbet

FROZEN RAINBOW PÂTÉ

This refreshing summer dessert has it all — it's simple to prepare, looks beautiful and tastes superb! Make it early in the day or the night before.

1/2	tub (1 L) PC Passion Fruit Sherbet	1/2
1/2	tub (1 L) PC Key Lime Sherbet	1/2
1/2	tub (1 L) PC Raspberry Sherbet	1/2
1/2	tub (1 L) PC Mango Sherbet	1/2
	Fresh berries, mint sprigs	

• Line a 9-inch (2 L) loaf pan with parchment or waxed paper.

• Allow passion fruit sherbet to soften slightly. Spread evenly along bottom of loaf pan; use a spoon or knife dipped in hot water to smooth surface. Cover with plastic wrap and place in freezer until firm, about 30 minutes.

• Repeat procedure with key lime and raspberry sherbets, allowing each layer to freeze thoroughly before adding the next. Be sure to spread sherbets gently to avoid disturbing the previous layer.

• Add mango sherbet, cover pan with plastic wrap and freeze for 2 to 4 hours or overnight.

• Remove pâté from pan and place on dessert platter. Using a hot knife, cut into 1/2-inch (1 cm) slices. Garnish with fresh berries and mint sprigs.

Makes 8 to 10 servings.

LOUIS DE BUADE FRONTENAC (1622-1698), GOVERNOR OF NEW FRANCE, KEPT UP ON THE LATEST FOOD TRENDS. ONCE, WHEN ICES WERE THE RAGE IN PARIS, HE HAD HIS COOK PREPARE SOME OF EVERY COLOR FOR A DINNER HE HOSTED IN QUEBEC CITY FOR VISITING INDIAN CHIEFS. (ALAS, FOOD ALONE DOES NOT A RELATIONSHIP MAKE. TODAY, FRONTENAC IS REMEMBERED MORE FOR DAMAGING THE FUR TRADE THAN HIS GOURMET TASTES.)

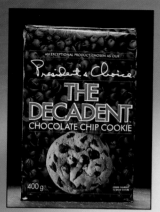

PC The Decadent
Chocolate Chip Cookies

The song with the longest title was written in 1941: "I'm Looking for a Guy Who Plays Alto and Baritone and Doubles on a Clarinet and Wears a Size Thirty-Seven Suit." Now that's long-winded! But it was a hit, as were these ice cream sandwiches when we sampled them in our test kitchen. They're made with our chocolate fudge crackle ice cream, chocolate chip cookies and bittersweet chocolate bar from France — which brings together in one place a few President's Choice products with names that could set their own records for length. And, of course, taste.

THE DECADENT ICE CREAM SANDWICH

These delectable treats flaunt their hand-made charm with a chocolate "ledge" that forms when the chocolate from the dipped sandwiches pools slightly during the final freezing.

12	scoops PC The Decadent Chocolate Fudge Crackle Ice Cream or PC Beyond Decadence Dutch Chocolate Chocolate Fudge Crackle Ice Cream, slightly softened	12
24	PC The Decadent Chocolate Chip Cookies	24
1/2	bar (17.6 oz/500 g) PC Bittersweet Rich Dark Chocolate	1/2

• Place a scoop of ice cream between 2 cookies. Press cookies firmly together to form sandwich; ice cream should extend to edge of cookies. Use knife or spatula to smooth edge of ice cream or fill in any gaps, if necessary. Repeat with remaining cookies and ice cream.

• Arrange sandwiches on waxed paper-lined baking sheet, cover loosely with waxed paper and freeze until firm, about 1 to 2 hours (not longer than 4 hours or cookies may get soggy).

• In top of double boiler over hot water, melt chocolate until smooth. Dip half of each frozen ice cream sandwich into melted chocolate; return to baking sheet and freeze for 5 to 10 minutes until set.

Makes 12 sandwiches.

ROOT BEER FLOAT

During the '50s, soda jerks called root beer with ice cream a "root beer bottom!"

2	scoops PC The Decadent Chocolate Fudge Crackle Ice Cream	2
1 cup	or more PC Root Beer, chilled	250 mL

• Place ice cream in tall glass. Fill with root beer.

Makes 1 serving.

My advice to you is not to inquire why or whither, but just enjoy your ice cream while it's on your plate.

— Thornton Wilder
(1897-1975)

PC The Decadent
Chocolate Fudge Crackle
Ice Cream

If you're looking for a banana split that defies tradition, this is it. The salsa topping — a blend of tropical fruits, red pepper and sweet Vidalia onion(!) — is zesty and refreshing atop our creamy chocolate fudge crackle ice cream and lightly grilled bananas. One tip: Be sure to use a sweet onion. If you can't find a Vidalia, substitute Maui or Texas 1015. The salsa should be piquant, not pungent.

GRILLED BANANA SPLIT WITH TROPICAL FRUIT SALSA

When test kitchen chef Ted Reader waxed eloquent about this new wave dessert, everyone was intrigued — but slow to pick up a spoon. A few minutes later, the dish was licked clean and everyone was singing the "Banana Boat Song," so to speak! (Day-O, Da-a-ay-O!) Serve any leftover salsa with grilled fish or poultry.

6	bananas, with peel on	6
1	tub (2 L) PC The Decadent Chocolate Fudge Crackle Ice Cream	1
3/4 cup	PC Gourmet Chocolate Ice Cream & Dessert Topping	175 mL
3/4 cup	PC Gourmet Butterscotch Ice Cream & Dessert Topping	175 mL
1 cup	whipping cream, whipped	250 mL
Tropical Fruit Salsa:		
1	papaya, peeled and diced	1
1	mango, peeled and diced	1
1/2	small pineapple, peeled and diced	1/2
1/2	red bell pepper, diced	1/2
2 to 3 tbsp	finely chopped Vidalia or other sweet onion	30 to 45 mL
2 tbsp	PC Key West Lime Juice	25 mL
2 tbsp	chopped fresh coriander	25 mL
1 to 2 tsp	PC Louisiana Hot Sauce	5 to 10 mL

♦ Prepare Tropical Fruit Salsa first: Mix together papaya, mango, pineapple, red pepper and onion. Add lime juice, coriander and Louisiana hot sauce. Mix well. Chill until serving.

♦ On lightly greased grill over medium-high heat, grill bananas until skin starts to split. Peel and cut bananas in half lengthwise.

♦ To assemble: Place 2 banana halves in each of 6 dessert boats or on individual dessert plates. Top with 3 scoops of ice cream. Spoon Tropical Fruit Salsa over centre scoop of ice cream. Drizzle chocolate topping over one of end scoops, butterscotch over remaining scoop.

♦ Top with whipped cream.

Makes 6 servings.

PC 30% Fruit, Nuts and Seeds Muesli

SERVE THESE AT THE END OF A MEAL WITH SORBET AND FRESH OR GRILLED FRUIT — OR SIMPLY WITH VIN SANTO (OR OTHER DESSERT WINE) OR ESPRESSO. THEY'RE ALSO A SUPERB ACCOMPANIMENT TO YOUR MORNING COFFEE. THE LEMON FLAVOR IS STRONGEST THE DAY THEY ARE MADE.

Perhaps there should be a museum dedicated to the original biscuits of the world, lest we forget their origin. The word biscuit comes from the French *bis-cuit*, which means twice cooked. ("Cookie" comes from the Dutch word *koekje*, or little cake.) The second baking renders genuine biscuits golden brown and irresistibly crunchy.

German *zweiback* (it also means twice-baked) is one example of the genre, as are toasted slices of the Spanish sponge cake, *bizcochi*. But our mouths are inclined to wrap themselves around an Italian biscotti, perhaps the most delectable and satisfying cookie ever devised.

MUESLI BISCOTTI

These biscuits are easy to consume in quantity. The only reason we can't guarantee long storage is that it's virtually impossible to stop eating them.

2 cups	PC 30% Fruit, Nuts and Seeds Muesli	500 mL
1 cup	all-purpose flour	250 mL
2/3 cup	granulated sugar	150 mL
1 tsp	grated lemon rind	5 mL
3/4 tsp	baking powder	4 mL
Pinch	salt	Pinch
1/4 cup	cold PC Unsalted Normandy-Style Cultured Butter, cut in pieces	50 mL
2	eggs, lightly beaten	2
1 tsp	pure vanilla extract	5 mL

• Place muesli in food processor and pulse on and off a few times just to break up large pieces. Set aside.
• In food processor, combine flour, sugar, lemon rind, baking powder and salt; pulse on and off a few times to blend. Add butter and pulse on and off just until mixture resembles coarse meal; do not overprocess.
• Add eggs and vanilla and process a few seconds just until blended.
• Transfer dough to mixing bowl. Stir in muesli until blended.
• Divide dough into three pieces. Shape each piece into a loaf that is about 1¼ inches (3 cm) high and 4 inches (10 cm) wide. Seal in plastic wrap and refrigerate for 1 to 2 hours or longer.
• Remove plastic wrap and place on lightly buttered baking sheet. Bake in 350°F (180°C) oven for 20 minutes. Remove from oven and let rest a few minutes until cool enough to handle.
• Transfer to cutting board. Using serrated knife, cut crosswise into ½-inch (1 cm) slices. Arrange slices on baking sheet and bake another 12 minutes or until biscotti are firm and golden brown. Let cool on rack.
Makes 12 to 16 biscotti.

Five Fabulous Refreshers, from left: Killer Iced Coffee, Tropical Smoothie, Sunshine Iced Tea (in pitcher and goblet), Salt Spring Punch and Salsa Zinger. Turn page for recipes.

SALT SPRING PUNCH

The recipe for this exquisitely refreshing beverage comes from the Salt Spring Centre in British Columbia. It appeared in Salt Spring Island Cooking: Vegetarian Recipes from the Salt Spring Centre *and was contributed by Kalpana, a graphic artist from a sister yoga facility in California. (Obviously, her talents lie in the kitchen as well!)*

With the kind permission of the authors, Rodney Polden and Pamela Thornley, and Macmillan Canada, we reproduce Kalpana's recipe here, using President's Choice products. It drew raves from cookbook editor Carol White, who drained several glasses one afternoon when temperatures were soaring!

8 cups	boiling water	2 L
2	PC Mint Refresher Tea Bags	2
2	PC Red Thriller Tea Bags	2
1½ cups	pineapple juice	375 mL
1½ cups	PC Canada Fancy Unsweetened Pure Apple Juice	375 mL
	Juice of 1 lemon	
2 to 3 tbsp	PC Premium Alfalfa Honey	30 to 45 mL
	Ice cubes	

• Pour boiling water over mint refresher and red thriller tea bags and let steep for about 5 minutes. Remove tea bags.
• Stir in pineapple juice, apple juice, lemon juice and honey. Chill and serve over ice.
Makes 8 to 10 servings.

TROPICAL SMOOTHIE

On hot summer mornings when you're pressed for time, make this sustaining and refreshing beverage for breakfast.

1	ripe mango, peeled and coarsely chopped	1
1	ripe banana, coarsely chopped	1
1 cup	PC 100% Pure Orange Juice (Not From Concentrate)	250 mL
1 tbsp	PC Premium Alfalfa Honey	15 mL
	Juice of ½ lemon	
6	(approx.) ice cubes	6

• In blender or food processor, combine mango, banana, orange juice, honey and lemon juice. Add ice cubes and process until thick and frothy.
Makes 2 servings.

PC Mint Refresher and Red Thriller Tea Bags

▲

PUNCH HAS ITS ORIGINS IN 17TH CENTURY INDIA. THE NAME COMES FROM THE HINDI WORD *PANCH*, MEANING "FIVE," SINCE PUNCH ORIGINALLY HAD FIVE INGREDIENTS: TEA, SPIRITS, LEMON JUICE, SUGAR AND SPICE. BRITISH MERCHANTS SPREAD THE IDEA TO ENGLAND, THE WEST INDIES AND THE COLONIES. IN CANADA, PUNCH WAS SERVED IN TAVERNS AND COFFEE HOUSES IN THE 18TH AND 19TH CENTURIES.

▼

SUNSHINE ICED TEA

The nightmare for early farm wives was cooking on wood stoves in the heat of summer for haying crews of as many as 30 or 40! Sun tea was one of the strategies they devised to beat the heat, and it became the preferred method for making tea wherever the sun shone long and hard. Instead of heating up the kettle, homesteaders would set the pitcher on a window ledge and let the tea brew all afternoon in the hot sun. For a delicious variation, mix with equal parts of chilled pineapple juice.

8	bags President's Blend Orange Pekoe Tea	8
6 cups	cold water	1.5 L
1/4 cup	PC Premium Alfalfa Honey	60 mL
1/4 cup	fresh lemon juice	60 mL
	Ice cubes	
	Lemon slices	

• Place tea bags in large glass jar with tight-fitting lid. Add water, secure lid in place and place outdoors in the sun or in front of a sunny window for a few hours or, if you're feeling especially lazy, until the mood strikes you.
• Stir in honey and lemon juice and refrigerate until chilled.
• Serve in tall glasses over ice. Garnish with lemon slices.

Makes 4 to 6 servings.

KILLER ICED COFFEE

This sensational beverage appeared in our first President's Choice cookbook, but everyone felt it deserved a repeat performance. If you don't have an espresso machine, use a plunger-type coffee maker or prepare double strength coffee in your drip pot.

1 cup	PC Sweetened Condensed Milk	250 mL
9 to 12	ice cubes	9 to 12
4 cups	(approx.) freshly brewed President's Blend Espresso Coffee	1 L

• Pour condensed milk into each of 4 glasses. Add ice cubes to each and fill to the top with espresso coffee. Stir well and serve immediately.

Makes 4 servings.

FROTHY SALSA ZINGER

HERE'S HOW TO MAKE THIS LOW-CALORIE REFRESHER: IN FOOD PROCESSOR OR BLENDER, COMBINE 1 CUP (250 mL) CHILLED PC TOMATO CLAM COCKTAIL, 1 CUP (250 mL) CHILLED PC LA ELECCIÓN DEL PRESIDENTE EXTRA-CHUNKY MILD SALSA PICANTE AND 1/2 CUP (125 mL) COLD WATER. PULSE ON AND OFF A FEW TIMES UNTIL FROTHY. SERVE OVER ICE. MAKES 2 SERVINGS.

BARBECUE BASICS

The dangerous person in the kitchen is the one who goes rigidly by weights, measurements, thermometers and scales.

— Marcel Boulestin

Food writer Marcel Boulestin could have been commenting on barbecue in particular, because more than any other form of cooking, grilling hones your instincts. Grilling forces you to disregard the rules about what to cook when, where, and for how long. You barbecue because the mood strikes, you choose the foods you and your family most enjoy, and you cook for as long as your senses tell you to.

One becomes a grill master by first reading up on barbecue (don't underestimate the importance of the grill manufacturer's manual) and then getting down to the actual cooking.

What a cookbook about barbecue can advise you on, among other things, are the tools of the trade, as it were. It goes without saying that the quality of ingredients and temperature of the fire are of primary importance, but there are many accoutrements that make life easier for the barbecuer. Be sure to clear a space for them. Here, in no particular order, are some that we find invaluable:

- long-bladed spatula
- extra-long spring-loaded tongs (if you build charcoal fires, get a second set for moving briquets)
- long-handled fork
- long-handled natural bristle basting brush
- heavy-duty fireproof mitts
- heavy saucepan (for cooking on side burner or on top of grill)
- glass, porcelain or stainless steel pan for marinating (avoid aluminum; it reacts with certain foods)
- instant-read meat thermometer
- wire grill basket
- grill topper (keeps small foods from falling through the grill; usually made of metal — some are porcelain-coated)
- V-shaped barbecue rack (for slow cooking poultry and roasts; allows for even cooking without turning)
- heavy-duty aluminum foil
- wire brush or combination brush-and-scraper for cleaning grill

- cloth or paper towelling moistened with vegetable oil or a vegetable oil cooking spray to grease grill rack and prevent food from sticking
- spray bottle filled with water to control flare-ups
- metal or wooden skewers (wooden skewers should be soaked in water for at least 30 minutes before using to prevent burning)
- for charcoal users: either an electric starter or chimney-style charcoal starter, also called a metal flue (they eliminate the need for chemical starters; chimney starters are especially useful for igniting extra briquets to add to an existing fire)
- for gas grill users: heavy-duty, full-length vinyl cover to protect your barbecue from the elements

Flavoring the Food

Flavoring agents can be wet or dry. If dry, they're called dusts or rubs; if wet, you're looking at a basic marinade or basting sauce.

Dry Rubs: As their name implies, these are dry agents that are rubbed liberally into foods to add flavor. They do not tenderize. Dried herbs, salt-free seasonings or seasoning blends, such as cajun, 5-spice or curry powder, are rubbed into the food a few hours before cooking to impart flavor. Some dry rubs are applied just before grilling to act as a thin coating and help seal in juices.

As a general rule, use 1 to 2 tablespoons (15 to 30 mL) of "dry rub" per pound (500 g) of meat, fish or poultry. Let stand 1 hour at room temperature. For stronger flavor, cover and let marinate in refrigerator for 2 to 3 hours or longer. Try rosemary with beef; mint, garlic and lemon peel with lamb; caraway or crushed juniper berries with pork; and basil, thyme or oregano with chicken.

Dusts: A dust is a sprinkling of flavor. It can be as simple as freshly ground black pepper. Or use your favorite seasonings, such as curry powder or dry mustard. Sprinkle or shake dusts lightly and evenly over the entire surface of the food before grilling.

Marinades: A marinade usually contains an acid ingredient, such as wine, vinegar or lemon juice (for tenderizing), oil (for lubricating) and spices (for flavoring). It can also be as simple as plain lemon juice. A marinade works by displacing the moisture in meat or fish, which means it tenderizes and flavors from the outside in. If left too long, however, flesh can break down and become mushy.

Lean fish can benefit from a light coating of oil and a sprinkling of chopped fresh or dried herbs. Save the tenderizing marinades (those containing wine, vinegar or yogurt) for firmer, more oily fish.

Marinate meat and poultry at room temperature for up to 2 hours or refrigerate in the marinade for up to 48 hours, turning occasionally. (Allow all refrigerated foods to warm to room temperature before cooking.) Fish and seafood require the briefest marinating period: No longer than 30 to 45 minutes in an acid-based mixture.

A plastic bag that can be tightly sealed is useful for marinating as it enables you to turn the package easily to ensure that all food surfaces come in contact with the marinade.

A basting sauce is applied to foods while they're on the grill. Many marinades double as basting sauces, such as our PC Memories of Hawaii Polynesian Sweet & Sour Marinade & Basting Sauce or Memories of Singapore Passion Fruit Sauce & Glaze. A quick, low-calorie basting sauce can be made with meat stock or chicken broth mixed with vinegar, lemon juice or apple cider and seasonings to taste.

MEAT THERMOMETERS

Use an instant-read meat thermometer for large cuts of meat or poultry. Insert it into the thickest part of the flesh, away from the bone. Food will continue to cook after it's taken off the grill. Most meats are juiciest when cooked rare to medium. Poultry should be cooked just until juices run clear and flesh is no longer pink. Here's a general guide to doneness based on internal temperature.

- **Rare:** 120°F (50°C)
- **Medium Rare:** 130°F (55°C)
- **Medium:** 140°F (60°C)
- **Medium Well:** 155°F (68°C)
- **Well Done:** 160°F (70°C)

Caution: Burgers should always be cooked until they are no longer pink inside, as ground meat can harbor microorganisms that are only destroyed by thorough cooking.

FAST COOKING

Fast cooking is recommended for poultry, fish fillets, burgers, chops, vegetables, skewered foods and steaks.

Use medium-high or high heat and keep lid up to let in oxygen, which enables the fire to burn faster and hotter. If you must close the lid, be sure vents are completely open. For more intense heat, lower grill rack or bank coals closer together.

Fast-Cooking Charcoal Fire: Start coals about 30 to 35 minutes ahead and let burn to a white ash. For an average fire that lasts about an hour, use 30 to 40 briquets, or enough to make a single layer that extends about 1 inch (2.5 cm) beyond the area covered by the food. Place food on grill and close lid; regulate heat with upper and lower vents. Don't close vents completely or the fire will die out for lack of oxygen. Add 8 to 10 briquets to the existing fire after about 30 minutes of cooking to maintain heat for about half an hour. Repeat as necessary every 30 minutes.

You can determine at a glance the intensity of a charcoal fire. At low heat, the coals will be thickly coated with ash. When the fire is medium-hot, most of the coals will be glowing and covered with ash. When the fire is hot, the coals will be barely covered with white ash.

Fast-Cooking Gas Fire: Before cooking, turn burners to highest setting and close lid. Let heat 5 minutes before adjusting temperature (or follow manufacturer's instructions). Medium-high heat is suitable for most grilling. After cooking, brush grill with wire brush, close lid and turn to high for 5 to 10 minutes to "burn off" traces of food.

SLOW COOKING

Slow cooking is recommended for whole roasts, turkeys, chickens, veal breast, game, lamb leg, pork roasts and beef roasts (e.g., chuck, rib, cross rib).

Also called indirect cooking, slow cooking is similar to oven cooking. The key is to maintain a fairly constant temperature. This is done by keeping the lid closed and regulating heat with vent holes. Open vents completely to increase heat, partially close to reduce heat. Instructions follow for setting up a slow-cooking fire for charcoal and gas barbecues.

Slow-Cooking Charcoal Fire: About 30 minutes ahead, light about 50 to 60 briquets and let burn down until they're covered with white ash. Bank coals on either side of grill and put foil drip tray in middle, below rack; or, for maximum heat, position drip tray in the middle of the grill and surround with briquets. For a slower fire, push all the briquets to one side of the grill and position drip tray on the opposite side. Put lightly oiled grill rack in place and position food over drip tray. Cook food with lid down and vents open. Refrain from lifting lid too often as this permits heat to escape.

Generally speaking, to maintain the heat, add briquets after the first 30 minutes of cooking time. Add about 10 to 12 briquets each half-hour for each half-hour of additional cooking time you require. Put them directly on top of the fire to ignite, or light them in a chimney-style charcoal starter put in an old pie pan or large clay saucer set on concrete; when ready, carefully pour them on the existing fire.

Slow-Cooking Gas Fire: You can cook on the top rack if the food fits the surface area. Before putting food on the rack, turn burners to high and close lid. Let heat for 5 minutes. Make foil drip tray slightly larger than the area covered by the food; position on grill below area where food will be placed. Place food on grill. Close lid, reduce temperature to low or medium, depending on heat required, and let cook.

For some roasts and ribs, more cooking surface is required so you will need to cook directly on the grill. Make a foil drip tray and place it on the lava rocks or ceramic briquets on one side of grill or, if you have three burners, in the centre of grill. Turn burners to high and close lid. Let heat for 5 minutes. When barbecue is hot, turn off burner where drip tray is positioned. Place food on grill over drip tray. Regulate heat with other burner(s).

Hand-Testing the Fire

Most grilling is done over medium to medium-high heat. To determine the heat of your fire, place your hand about 4 inches (10 cm) above the coals or lava rocks and calculate how long you can hold it there.

- 5 seconds: **Low**
- 4 seconds: **Medium**
- 3 seconds: **Medium-high**
- 2 seconds: **High**

Cooking with Foil

Have you ever wondered which side of the foil is supposed to face up? Contrary to popular belief, it doesn't matter. The heat reflectivity of the shiny side is close enough to that of the dull side that either side can face up or out.

Foil wrap is invaluable at a barbecue. You can use it to line kettle grills for easier cleanup, for wrapping fish fillets or vegetables that you want to cook in the embers, for making disposable drip pans and for tenting foods cooked on open grills to speed up cooking time.

FOR SAFETY'S SAKE

The idea is to start a fire in your grill, not your house, so please reacquaint yourself with safety tips whenever you plan to grill. Here are some important considerations.

- Don't barbecue in high winds.
- Keep grill well away from walls, shingled roofs, leaves, wood fences, dry grass, foliage or other potential fire hazards.
- Never move grill while hot.
- Never leave grill unattended, especially when lighting it.
- Use only commercially prepared fire-starters and use them only to start fires. Never add them to established fires or hot coals.
- Keep grill in level position at all times so there is no danger of it toppling over.
- Don't add self-starting briquets to a fire while food is cooking.
- Wear fireproof mitts or fireplace mitts. Fringed dish towels and pot holders can easily catch fire. As well, avoid wearing long, loose sleeves when grilling.
- Keep a spray bottle filled with water nearby at all times to control flare-ups or sparks. It's also advisable to keep grill within close proximity of a connected garden hose.
- When grill is not in use, disconnect it from its fuel source and turn off all control knobs.
- Store propane tanks outdoors — never in an enclosed area, like your home or garage.
- Remove ashes only after all the coals have completely burned down.
- Invest in a good-quality fire extinguisher and always keep it handy when grilling.